EMPOWERED
2022

WORDS ON FIRE

Edited By Daisy Job

First published in Great Britain in 2022 by:

Young Writers
Remus House
Coltsfoot Drive
Peterborough
PE2 9BF
Telephone: 01733 890066
Website: www.youngwriters.co.uk

All Rights Reserved
Book Design by Ashley Janson
© Copyright Contributors 2022
Softback ISBN 978-1-80459-076-8

Printed and bound in the UK by BookPrintingUK
Website: www.bookprintinguk.com
YB0510Z

⭐ FOREWORD ⭐

Since 1991, here at Young Writers we have celebrated the awesome power of creative writing, especially in young adults where it can serve as a vital method of expressing their emotions and views about the world around them. In every poem we see the effort and thought that each student published in this book has put into their work and by creating this anthology we hope to encourage them further with the ultimate goal of sparking a life-long love of writing.

Our latest competition for secondary school students, Empowered, challenged young writers to consider what was important to them. We wanted to give them a voice, the chance to express themselves freely and honestly, something which is so important for these young adults to feel confident and listened to. They could give an opinion, share a memory, consider a dilemma, impart advice or simply write about something they love. There were no restrictions on style or subject so you will find an anthology brimming with a variety of poetic styles and topics. We hope you find it as absorbing as we have.

We encourage young writers to express themselves and address subjects that matter to them, which sometimes means writing about sensitive or contentious topics. If you have been affected by any issues raised in this book, details on where to find help can be found at www.youngwriters.co.uk/info/other/contact-lines

✴ CONTENTS ✴

Bideford College, Bideford

Jasmin Vanstone	1
Daisy Williams (15)	2
Poppy Sojitra	4
Holly Stone	6
Chloe Webb	7
Holly Leather (13)	8
Ellie Deacon (12)	9
Kayne Willis (12)	10

Bishop Gore School, Sketty

Joseph Levy	11
Elliot Abrahams	12
Kiara Motoomull	14

Broomhill Bank School (North), Hextable

Shaun H	15
Kodi Ward	16
Leon Lindo-Gardiner (11)	20

Charles Darwin School, Biggin Hill

Rose Greiff (11)	21

Colchester Institute, Colchester

Jess Worrell (16)	22

Communication Specialist College Doncaster, Doncaster

Ellie-Rose Davis (18)	23

Compass Community School: Aylward Park, Leiston

Thelma Ikoza (15)	24

Cross And Passion College, Ballycastle

Tiarnan Staunton (14)	27

Deyes High School, Maghull

Olivia Baker (11)	28

Don Valley Academy, Scawthorpe

Kelsey Colbourne (14)	30

Doon Academy, Dalmellington

Brodie Logan (15)	32

Esher CE High School, Esher

Lily Sutton (14)	40
Sophia Hammond-Aziz (12)	42
Millie Gannon (12)	43

Exhall Grange School, Ash Green

Carmen McLellan (17)	44

Kings Langley School, Kings Langley

Juhi Gajjar (16)	47

Merchant Taylors' Girls' School, Crosby

Lauren Roseberry (15)	48

Murray Park Community School, Mickleover

Abel Sawyerr (12)	50

Newquay Tretherras, Newquay

Lily Pinkham (12)	51

North Cestrian School, Altrincham

Theodora T	52
Kiera Strathmore (11)	54
Angel C (13)	55

Northview House School, Kilbarchan

Taylor (16)	56
Zayden Vaughn Sharp (13)	57
Teigan Maria Davidson (13)	58
Deri-J	59

Northwood College For Girls (GDST), Northwood

Ava Breed (14)	60

Orchards Academy, Swanley

Alexa-Jane Calver (15)	61
Dana Balao Schoener (16)	62
Chloe Gregory (15)	65
Emma-Jane Langley (13)	66
Tamzin Doody (16)	70

Annabelle Law (11)	72
Ruby May Gomm (12)	74
Lewis Walford (12)	75
Azaria Peverley (11)	76
Isabelle Carter (13)	77
Rebecca Jones (12)	78
Demi Fisher (12)	79
Ronnie Webb (11)	80
Charlotte Loftus (11)	81
Julia Sibielska (12)	82
Lucy Coulson (15)	83

Robert Blake Science College, Bridgwater

Libby Boobyer	84
Violet Gainsford	85

Sacred Heart Grammar School, Newry

Orla Fullerton (13)	86
Amy Fitzpatrick (13)	88
Aebha Phillips (12)	89
Amy Fullerton (13)	90
Kate Boyd (13)	91
Iulia Zanfir (13)	92
Cara McCusker (12)	93
Kate Orr (13)	94

Sir Frederick Gibberd College, Harlow

Morgan Bonnage (13)	95
Caitlin (14)	96

St George Catholic College, Swaythling

Niamh Magee & Claudia Tombaccini-Maestro	97

St James' CE High School, Farnworth

Rosie-Anna Prior (13)	99
Melissa Bailey (13)	100

St John The Baptist's College, Portadown

Niamh McCann	102
Holly Preshur	106

St Robert Of Newminster, Fatfield

Olivia Groark (13)	107

Stockport School, Stockport

Mathilda Warren-O'Neill	109
Erin-Lily Taylor (13)	110

Stopsley High School, Luton

Storm Rogers (14)	112
Ali Kayani (14)	114
Milly Hawkins (14)	116
Safiyyah Jarral (12)	118
Mia Stratton (12)	120
Iris Bartlett (13)	121
Aryan Uddin (13)	122
Tahsiath Tanmi	124
Luke McCulloch (12)	125
Anushka Patel (14)	126
Sophie Croft (14)	128
Aliyah Hoque (11)	129
Lexie Dawson-Mannion (14)	130
Ava Mensah-Mahmud (12)	131
Tahsin Sayed (12)	132
Aimee Thrussell (12)	133
Evie Keeling (14)	134
Pawel Doruch (13)	135
Kam Reid (13)	136
Ibrahim Hossain (12)	137
Mahad Haider Afsheen (11)	138
Eshan Hussain (12)	139
Alonso Mangwende	140
Alecsandra Ciolan (11)	141
Alex Chapman (14)	142
Olatomiwa Osobu (12)	143
Iqra Islam (12)	144
Katie Davis (11)	145
Nikola Dadia (13)	146
Maja Laclak	147
Kiyana Henry (12)	148
Freddie Theron (13)	149
Mia Larsen (11)	150
Hasnain Qaisar (12)	151
Emily Booth (12)	152
Ehsan Hanif (14)	153

Stretford Grammar School, Manchester

Hannah Jones	154
Emmy Smith (12)	157
Sophie Allen	158
Ben Carroll (15)	160
Aya Yousif	162
Bisma Rizwan	164
Daniel Ghebreyesus (12)	166
Minahil Hussain (13)	168
Jouna Albaid (17)	170
William Murphy (15)	172
Divine Chijindu Udensi (15)	174
Fezaan Ali Hussain (14)	175
Mariya Alam (14)	176
Eva Carpenter (14)	178
Favour Osuagwu	180
William Boast Kemp (13)	182
Lola Heys	183
Yazan Naser Eddin (13)	184
Sofia Ahmed (16)	185
Olive Broom (12)	186
Shaker Darwazeh (14)	187
Kainaat Wahid (18)	188
Syed Ibrahim Ali (13)	189
James Swales (14)	190
Scarlett Moss	191

Dhillan Nagra (14)	192
Subhanullah Naseri (13)	193
Rory Kielty (15)	194
Saahil Malik	195
Ivan Flitcroft (17)	196
Esa Mohammed (12)	197
Ryan Buckley (12)	198
Nadia Basir (16)	199
Muhammad Tahoor Ali	200
Luca Cardilli-Ferry (13)	201
Daisy Wheadon	202
Kira Lee (13)	203
Hanifah Aslam (11)	204
Jack Styczen-O'Keefe (13)	205
Sofia Whitehouse (16)	206
Freya Scott (11)	207
Evan Lewis (13)	208
Reuben Quansah	209
Erin Mann (14)	210
Hibah Khan (11)	211
Jack Chell	212
James Osuh (12)	213
Harrison Ritchie (15)	214
Laura Goodyer (12)	215
Benjamin Hosford (12)	216
Sihaam Omar (13)	217
Syed Younus Hussain (12)	218
Oluchi Ezekiel (13)	219
Ronique Walker (11)	220
Kaj Middleton (13)	221
Oliver Hitchen (13)	222
Zoha Munir (15)	223
Ben Parsons (11)	224
Muhammad Abdulwahab (11)	225
Cohen Jackson (12)	226
Shaowen Xu (12)	227
Georgia Smith (16)	228
Ozzy Thorp (11)	229
Ali Sharfeden (17)	230
Ahmed Soomro (16)	231

THE POEMS

Something Wrong With Our Planet

People think they don't belong,
That they are freaks and God made them wrong,
But they will never see how much they make a difference.

People think that they can't be themselves,
They don't feel safe at home either,
Well, our world changes now,
So they can make a choice,
They need you to help them feel safe,
The next words are for people who discriminate others.

How would you feel?
Just think how they feel,
And how you treat them,
If the roles were reversed, how would you feel?
So, change the world for the better.

They are waiting for people to change the way they see them,
We are the change on this planet.

Jasmin Vanstone
Bideford College, Bideford

Dear Past Me

Dear past me,
I know you think that you're fine,
But you don't have to hide, your failings are mine,
And as much as I want to tell you
That your life will be full of success,
I cannot.
You will be victimised and sympathised,
Yet over the top, dramatised,
You'll be welcome,
But you won't belong.
I'm not saying
That our life is a misery,
There are things that we enjoy to do and enjoy to see,
We will grow together, and change so much,
But the only person we'll truly have is us.
So be kind,
Because through all the pain,
And all the tears we shed,
You have made it through the nights,
Where we thought it might be nice
To hide forever,
And never be found,
But it's worth it.
Because we got to be there,
For every birthday, every party,

Everything you wanted to see,
And if we haven't seen it yet,
Let me promise you this,
We will.
Because you deserve it.

Daisy Williams (15)
Bideford College, Bideford

Be The Change!

You talk about equality, freedom and fairness,
You tell us you've changed for the better not worse,
Then show us.

Show us why we don't have to look down on streets,
Show us why it's actually worth preparing for an interview,
Show us equality.
Is that too much to ask for?

We are done,
Done with the whistling, shouting and name calling,
Done with the unfairness of this sorry world,
You have no excuse,
So stop pretending.

You tied us up,
Like pets that are yours,
But you don't own us.
The rope you used is old and weak,
We will break free
We are breaking free.

The shackles of injustice are rusty,
The chains of inequality decaying,
Your restraints won't last any longer,
They made us stronger.

The world is rearranging,
You need to start changing,
The definition of this new world is undecided,
Help us define it.

Poppy Sojitra
Bideford College, Bideford

Who Am I?

Who am I?
Male, female, non-binary
He, she, they
Gay, straight, bi
So many boxes to choose from
Too many to count upon
People choosing who I can and cannot be
But they don't know what it's like to be me
I feel trapped in my mind, confused on who I am
I have to figure out the answer like I'm in an exam
So much pressure, so much pain
So much strain on my brain
It's having such an impact on me mentally
I'm starting to feel like I can't have an identity
So here I am asking once again because the answer is always a lie
Once again, I ask
Who am I?

Holly Stone
Bideford College, Bideford

The Earth Is At Stake

Our world is collapsing,
we need to act now, if not now
it will affect our future.
We are trying our best
but it is not enough,
still litter is multiplying with the nasty greenhouse gases,
that we humans produce.
Once it was natural and safe
but now it's unstable and on the rage.
You could try to protest like you have
done before
to bring people
to help our planet,
but as we know the greenhouse gases have increased.
I do not want to leave this planet
that God has given us,
so we need to act now.
It is now
or never!

Chloe Webb
Bideford College, Bideford

Feminists Don't Just Like Glitter And Pink

Feminists don't just like glitter and pink
They are much more than you think

They are society changers
Strong campaigners
They are doing what's right
And they will put up a fight

They are powerful
And purposeful
They will stop at no limits
Whether it takes years or minutes

They are strong-willed
And incredibly skilled
They try their best
And protest to complete their quest

So feminists don't just like glitter and pink
They are so much more than you think.

Holly Leather (13)
Bideford College, Bideford

Put An End To Bullying

The tears,
the fears,
the emotion and stress,
being bullied,
is one of life's tests,
it happened to me,
it can happen to you,
so never let someone tell you what to do,
your anger takes over,
you want to fight back,
people make fun of you,
and you feel there is nothing you can do,
they do it to make themselves proud,
usually in front of a crowd,
and it is not just you,
it is others too,
so, let's put an end to this while we can,
and together we can make a plan.

Ellie Deacon (12)
Bideford College, Bideford

Losing It All

I had friends and joy,
And a cool school,
Then I lost them all,
Because my dad stood tall.
This was not cool,
And I lost my school,
I moved far away,
But I did not give up for a day.
In fact, I kept my way,
I made a new friend,
Who kept the sadness at bay,
We went to play,
And had a happy day.

Kayne Willis (12)
Bideford College, Bideford

Golden Sunlight

So far, so long
I have been without your presence,
I have been without hearing your laughter,
Without seeing your smile.

The sun gleaming on your golden hair,
The waves crashing upon the sand
As we talk.

The day you left
The sun was hidden behind the clouds,
And our eyes linked one last time
While your smile was the only sunlight to be found.

Joseph Levy
Bishop Gore School, Sketty

Here And There

The road is wrought of iron and wood,
Leading far south away, away,
Away from green and blue and the warm sun above,
To Flanders fields,
Where the wicked wind blows.

Trees, forests and hills come and go,
Disappearing as fast as they came,
Every time the steam whistle blows,
It announces the journey close to its end,
An end to the trees and perhaps an end for me.

At last we reach the great plain of blue,
That stretches from here to there,
I remember as a boy I used to ride that field,
In a boat with room for two,
Now I sail with two thousand.

The birds and beasts are loud at home,
Calling from dusk to dawn,
Here is the sharp whine of a skinny dog,
And the grunt of a horse,
As much a soldier as I.

There are no fields here untouched,
Like those I see at home,
The animals lie dead on the roadside,

Nature has been sacrificed for bombs and guns,
And humanity has been lost too.

Elliot Abrahams
Bishop Gore School, Sketty

Past Feelings

There are times
where I wish I had not met you

But in my inmost heart
I'm so relieved
to have found you

I discovered
a conspicuous type of
love

You made me feel
a lot of things
that I've never encountered

I am thrilled we coincidentally
met
many times
and I hope to see you
again.

Kiara Motoomull
Bishop Gore School, Sketty

Oxygen Thief

Every time I see myself in the mirror, I often take a second to stare and then move on with my day.
When I was younger, I remember staring without moving on. Staring for hours trying to figure out why the face staring back at me would scare me so much.
Pushing and pulling its face like clay, hoping it'd set.
I looked for zippers and seams along its skin to crawl out.
I forget this face.
After sixteen years, I know I'm just a spy intruding on someone else's mind.
I often find myself picking up the pieces they leave behind when I wake up like broken promises and times they weren't kind, bruises and scabs, tear stains on my cheek.
A spark of a memory ignites but it isn't mine, I don't exactly know how it happened but maybe I will like all those other times I stared at my face and remembered it with grief.
Sometimes I think I'd be better off being blind but then that would be scarring someone else's eyes.
I am breathing but these are not my lungs and with every breath I reap but don't sow.
Who am I without this body? Am I just a consciousness that can't help but feel guilty in being conscious or a husk?
Regardless, one thing is for sure.
I'm
Truly,
An oxygen thief.

Shaun H
Broomhill Bank School (North), Hextable

Lord Of The Rings Fellowship Of The Ring

One ring to rule them all
Wields armour and very tall
An army of elf and mankind
The ring taken and not to find
The king stole then became evil and a liar
He died and the ring was taken by a hobbit from the shire

In a field with farms and flowers
A village shy of weapons and towers
Small people with big feet
A hobbit and a wizard would soon meet
A world of adventure is what a boy loves to admire
As a wise wizard made his way to the Shire

As Frodo Baggins welcomed the grey wizard into the village
Gandalf worried for an orc attack more than a pillage
As they rode past hills, domed houses and people strumming string
The wizard met with Bilbo the bearer of the ring
The ring must be destroyed, and stakes were now higher
So, the mission must be left to Frodo of the Shire

Frodo was accompanied by his friend Sam
Someone who craved beef steak and ham
They met with two friends, Merry and Pippin on farm

As they joined the adventure not caring for the harm
They entered the woods which revealed a hooded, dark figure
They hid behind a log, not moving of fear to be a trigger

Gandalf rode to Saruman the White, an old friend
Not knowing that the two wizards' friendship would soon end
Out from the tower came the wizard with white hair and a white beard
Although them both being one of the five Saruman embarrassed what Gandalf feared
Both fought against and for Sauron the dark lord
Gandalf was imprisoned and was able to see the huge orc horde

As the hobbits settled in a nearby village
The dark figures, looking for the ring, prepared to pillage
A man called Aragon protected them with his sword
Big eagles saved Gandalf as the orcs roared
They all went to the elves to decide on the ring
Elves were great beings, pointy-eared and tall, they were great with bows and also could sing

All races were there, hobbits, elves, men and stubby dwarves
A common enemy had risen, orcs, dark, black and evil and riding wolves
The fellowship was made, and they all set out on the mission
The group made of all races, between the elf and the dwarf there was division

Four new members, first Gimli the dwarf, ginger, stubborn and hates to be thrown
Aragon, a human, dark hair, short beard and brave and for some of his life he was alone

There was an elf, Legolas, fair and blonde and has lots of skill
Boromir, a selfish man who wants the ring for his kingdom and for that he will kill
They headed through a mountain to pass
They discovered it was an abandoned fortress of dwarves digging diamond, steel and brass
Pippin dropped a helmet in a deep well
As hundreds of orcs marched and attacked and began to roar and yell

The fellowship ran to a bridge that was very thin and narrow
Suddenly a huge burning flame came rushing towards them and it was not an arrow
The monster was massive and burning like the sun
Gandalf stood still and told the others to run
Gandalf and monster fought, and they both fell and died
The fellowship was sad, and Frodo cried

They went to another kingdom of elves to rest
There was one from out of all she was the best
Galadriel, eyes like stars, thousands of years old
Voice like music and hair like gold
She called Frodo and showed him a hallucination
If he didn't destroy the ring there would be horror, death and orcs in every nation

The fellowship went through a forest and in the distance, they saw a figure
It was a group of Uruk-hai orcs but stronger, taller and bigger
They fought valiantly but Boromir fell
Frodo and Sam went alone to Mordor for a journey like hell
Pippin and Merry got taken by the Uruk-hai
The other three went after them, everyone must be careful as they all could die.

Kodi Ward
Broomhill Bank School (North), Hextable

Leon's London

Born south-east of the river where most of my family are from. Including my two grandads, John and John.

In south-east London, Lewisham to be exact, where the foods are exotic and the markets are packed.

Music, music all around, is that my cousin I can hear? His name is Tyrone Lindo, but Big Narstie people cheer.

People from all parts of the world, living in one place, this is my London this is my space.

Buildings new and old, big and tall where people work and live, London is a great big city that has a lot to give.

Leon Lindo-Gardiner (11)
Broomhill Bank School (North), Hextable

Anxiety

Cries falling on deaf ears,
I'm screaming and no one can see,
Blank face, wide eyes,
I can't be what I want to be,
I'm alone with my fears,
Cries falling on deaf ears.

Creatures creeping in the night,
I'm stuck in a space as they surround me,
Cold hands, in place,
Close my eyes, maybe they'll go and flee,
I'm alone, fighting my fight,
Creatures creeping in the night.

Fake smile is on,
My mask is there and I'll never be free,
My grin, not really there,
I want to cry, why can no one see?
I'm alone, always alone,
Fake smile is on.

People's hands appear,
They see that I'm screaming, feel like a banshee,
Good eyes, kind face,
I might be the roots but they are the tree,
I'm not alone, no fear,
People's hands appear.

Rose Greiff (11)
Charles Darwin School, Biggin Hill

What Then?

It's like a forest, with chirping birds, with the sun shining down.
Then you get to a fork in the road,
One leading to a dark and cold forest, the other is peaceful.
And when you panic about it, you go down the dark path,
It's lonely and cold and you're afraid.
But you think about what Churchill says if you're going through hell, keep going.
And then you run and you keep running and it's never-ending.
It's like a rope, that wraps around you tight and finally
You're out.
It's a panic attack, and you can't breathe and you're finally with the world.
Until something bad happens, then you have to do it all over again.
But what if you're tired of being alone, in the dark part of the forest?
What then?

Jess Worrell (16)
Colchester Institute, Colchester

Empower

Lizzie walked into the massive classroom and her mind started going wild with all the anxiety she felt as soon as she set foot into the car park.
As all eyes turned toward her
She felt as if she was being suffocated.
The more they watched her as she moved to give her new college teacher her late note, the less empowered Lizzie felt.
Lizzie's mother had always said, "No matter what, always believe in yourself."
Mr Clarkson simply directed Lizzie to her seat and continued with a lesson, not bothering to read the note.
The work set had Lizzie's mind spinning out of control.
Lizzie's anxiety built up inside her like a boiling pot about to explode, a volcano.
A knock on the door brought Lizzie back to reality, as everyone looked
They saw an elegant young man named Marco.
Lizzie felt calm as this man spoke to her teacher and then sat next to Lizzie.
Marco explained that he was there to assist her in any way required.
The next day everything seemed so much easier.
With the help of Lizzie's kind and patient SENs officer, as they were called in this college, each day was calmer.
Marco helped Lizzie to feel empowered.

Ellie-Rose Davis (18)
Communication Specialist College Doncaster, Doncaster

The Struggles Of Life As A Teenager

You've got a voice, so don't you dare stay silent
Make some noise and remember it's a choice
What you choose to do will shape how fast you move or even if you lose
So, stop wasting your time because time is all we got,
Because once you lose time, it's gone and there is nothing more

Us kids of these days are not okay, are in so much pain
We feel shame of the past and we show that in our scars
The scars buried deep within us, on our arms
Our chests, our stomachs, the thighs and under our collars

Is it sane that so many of us have already died in vain?
The thoughts to end it all deep inside our brains, and why? you adults ask
Because we feel like no one can mend it

And though we don't share the same blood
You're my sister and I love you that's the truth
Sisters at heart.
I laid next to you while you cried and I told you it would be alright
But where are you now? You're forever gone,
Dancing in the sky while we all mourn
Here on earth we all cry and why? Because it wasn't your time

But it's the bad people who made you die
They lied to you,
You're amazing,
It's just sad you didn't realise
But now we are all in pain and it's a shame the people who hurt you made you die in vain
but RIP because I'm glad you no longer feel the shame you felt, what they put on you, now rest in eternity
I hope to see you soon

So many of us feel the need to hurt us, but do you know why?
You don't want to because the reasons are unheard of

They made you want to die
So now it's time to rest
Remember to rest easy
For you will always be the best

It's all so sad, we are all lost at heart
The words deep inside of us now shape who we become
But only once you're dead,
We will know what's really gone

Dreams I've got dreams, but now let's be real
Dreams.
Will we ever achieve our dreams? Well let's just wait and see and only if we stop the greed
Think about us and also about others
For only if we stop hurting us and stop popping dots

Only then we will realise
We are enough to keep

So, when we all get to the end of the road and some of us get old
We will know if life was really
What we all got told.

Thelma Ikoza (15)
Compass Community School: Aylward Park, Leiston

My Hurling Story

The strike of a ball, the roar of the crowd,
The loud clash of the hurl.
Cold blood runs down my hand
But the adrenaline pumps through my body
As I battle on through the tackle.
Boom! Goal!
The back of the net shakes as the crowd roars
And cheers me on with my teammates.
The final whistle blows
As my excitement explodes!
The lift of the cup:
This moment I will forever treasure.

Tiarnan Staunton (14)
Cross And Passion College, Ballycastle

Shameless

Shame,
It's something we all have,
Whether it's for lying,
Or copying on a test,
But to be ashamed of yourself,
Well, there is no point in that,
Is there!

We are all different,
That's good,
I know that as a fact,
Sometimes people think that's bad,
It isn't
It's your life
Your rules
Even if parents say otherwise.

    S hame shouldn't exist
    H ow does it? I don't know.
    A nyway,
    M aybe you'll be scared to say who you are
    E ven scared to let yourself out of your shell
    L ove is important
    E specially when you need to love yourself
    S o, take time
    S how the world you!

Now the first letter of the last nine lines spell out shameless
Because that's what you should feel
Shameless to be *you!*

Olivia Baker (11)
Deyes High School, Maghull

Loneliness Is A State Of Mind

I feel darkness spreading through my veins.
I feel shadows thickening my blood.

My personality used to be bright
But now the dark's on the attack.
My surroundings once were daylight, now
They've become a pool of black.
I've used every ounce of strength
I have, just to drain light back.

Tears prick down my face with excruciating pain.
Face burns like flames flickering from the fire.
Stomach churns like emotions mixing.
Insides flip outside my atmosphere.

Nail bites, an addiction I will never get over.
Cower away in my hood hoping to not be seen.
I draw on my strength but my strength is failing
To light even the smallest of candles in me.

Tongue bites feel like I'm eating my insides,
In pictures I smiled so no one would worry.
All my feelings just run away and hide.
Don't want people to talk so emotions stay buried.

I hear my heartbeat heavy as the attack reaches its crushed end.
I feel my legs trembling and struggling to hold my balance.
I see a blur of vision and don't even spot the tiniest of light.
But I realise something, before anxiety's crescendo...

My behaviour changes? No
My personality changes? No
My self changes? No
Am I shown the reality? Yes

The emotions that I thought I would never face.
I faced.
The panics that I thought I would never face.
I faced.
The anxiety that I thought I would never face.
I faced.
The depression that I thought I would never face.
I faced.
The help I no longer wanted.
I got.
The rights I no longer wanted.
I demanded.

I am empowered to spread positivity and kindness.
I am empowered to stop negativity and selfishness.
I am empowered to help fight for mental health.

Kelsey Colbourne (14)
Don Valley Academy, Scawthorpe

A Series Of Me

Tattoo

I was born with a word tattooed across my forehead,
A word that would hold me back and weigh me down like pockets full of lead,
This word I did not have a say in,
But it would dictate the way I should be playing,
The way I should be saying my words, my word,
How I hated this word,
And I could tell you right from the start that this word shouldn't be there,
But I never tried to replace it,
I tried to embrace it so people wouldn't stare,
Some days I dressed as the part I was given at birth,
Other days I listened to my heart and knew what I was worth,
But for most of my life I didn't know,
That, one day I could be free of this tattoo I hated,
Maybe not completely free,
As I live in a world where people still try to read tattoos that are faded,
But for the people who really loved me and the people who really cared,
I could ask them to forget this word that declared something I'm not,
And in time they forgot,
I was born with a word tattooed across my forehead,

And I know you might still see remnants, know that these never represent
Who I am, who I'm going to be,
Because I was never a girl,
I've always just been me...
Or I will be when this curse is removed...

Curse

It's a 'girl' *they* said,
But, from day one, *they* were wrong
Sister/daughter/she and her,
That's all I heard for so long.
Put makeup on and wear a dress
That's how I'd find a man... right?
Pink is my favourite colour
But... but why? Isn't liking blue alright?
That's not for girls!
But since when did clothes have gender?
Grow out your hair long
But what if I like it shorter?
You see, the body that you see is not who I am
I was born a girl but, believe me, looks can be deceiving,
I'm sorry that I cannot be your daughter/sister/aunt or wife...
But I can be an amazing son/brother/uncle or husband.
So please let me reintroduce myself

As he and him
Because since day one *they* were wrong.

What I see

I frowned at the boy in the mirror,
His long hair was nothing like the short fluffy hair he desperately desired, he didn't look handsome.
His high-pitched voice was nothing like the deep, raspy voice he yearned for, his voice sounded too girly,
His body was hidden with a hoodie that was far too big for him, covering all his flaws and imperfections,
Tears were streaming down his face as he violently cried at the sight before him. How pathetic, right?
He looked so horrendous trapped in a body that didn't even belong to him,
And that boy is me.

What you see

You saw the same hair,
The same eyes
The same name
The same face
But where you see beauty,
I see a curse.
Being trapped in a body,
That it doesn't feel like
With a name that is no longer me...

Dead name

I sit down in class
The teacher is about to take the register
I hate this part,
Name after name... 'dead name'
Ughh
I angrily walk out of class, slamming the door behind me,
I'm transgender and changed my name, what was so difficult to get?
I'm already so dysphoric, barely anyone supports me,
She does,
She never misgenders me,
She even sticks up for me when someone does,
What did I do to deserve her?
But I still go to the toilet floor crying, taking out a blade from my pocket to prune my skin...

Drought

Depression is like a dying flower,
You're not dead yet but you want to die,
You're still alive yet you don't feel alive,
You need to get better but to get better you need to grow, to grow you need water, both metaphorically and realistically,
The dying flower needs to be watered by someone so it can come back to life,

You may need someone to 'water' you to help you stay alive and see the positives in life,
It's okay to ask for help, it's okay to be 'watered'.

Until you drown...

Drowning in my own skin while you watch blind,
My screams are muffled by the water above,
You tell me you understand,
Yet if you did why am I here?
And don't you dare tell me you care when you watch me fall into the deep dark waters, again.

Deep dark tears

I cried in my room,
Holding in the tears as small hiccups leave my mouth,
Why can't I be a boy?
I want the hair,
The lips,
The eyes,
The face,
I want to have that deep voice that everyone just melts over when they hear,
I suddenly started crying harder,
Why did I cry harder?
Oh right,
Because I realised,
That I cannot ever be a true boy like the others.

He's fine

He's fine,
But his voice is broken
Dried tears burn his soft, delicate skin,
He's fine,
But it's so hot out he wears hoodies in the blazing sun,
He's fine,
But his wrists ache
He wears too many chains to count,
He's fine,
But for the last time tears mix with blood on the tiled floor,
Maybe now they will care.

He's not fine

Rib breaking, years waiting yet still perceived as a girl.
Looked down upon by society for simply being myself,
I didn't choose this body, why would anyone choose this hell?
I wonder if it's worth it, I wonder if the dysphoria will stop, I wonder if I'll be accepted or if I'll never be free,
As quick as the thought comes it's far gone,
Looking down at my body, I need to be the man I am, I need this chest to be gone.
I'll never understand why, it isn't fair,
Yet I do know I can't live a lie, no matter what it may cause.
I'll be myself, I don't care if you stare.

He could have been fine

To find out at 15 that at 6 you know my phase of being a tomboy and not liking girl stuff was a symptom of childhood gender dysphoria,
But I was 11 before I even knew I was transgender,
I didn't know I could be something else... no one told me!
How unfair this life has been for you to blame me,
The 8,000 reconstructive chest surgery wouldn't have been necessary,
If you clicked at 6,
When I would run around without a shirt on because my younger brother got to and I always wanted to be just like him,
The last 5 years of living with gender dysphoria,
Because of a puberty that wasn't meant to be,
You haven't heard all the sick stuff,
You haven't seen the eyes as someone your age walks past screaming tranny,
In your own town where your parents moved you,
Small town will be fun they said.
But they were wrong

Hope
He will be fine

One day I'll be able to call this body home,
I've been building since day one
Limb by limb

Brick by brick

From the moment I could process the difference between me and her I've been planning
I knew one day if be strong enough to build a body that would mean something to me
No more bridge railing daydreams or endless sleep wishes
I'll rely on this body to be the reason why I'm still here, not why I don't want to be here
One day I'll be able to look in the mirror and say I love you,
And I'll mean it
5 years I've been working on the true me
And one day I'll finally not hate what I see.

Brodie Logan (15)
Doon Academy, Dalmellington

Masking

Every school day is pain
With nothing to lose or gain
She's exhausted from masking
With no one asking
If she's okay
Oh well she thinks, no one cares anyway.

Every second that draws near
The more she wants to disappear
Anxiety willing to drive her mad
She can't find the good, only the bad
The lights, the crowds, the shouting, so overwhelming
But everyone thinks she's just overreacting
The kids bully her and treat her like
In her life she's done nothing right
The teachers always notice
But act oblivious
The betrayal hits her like a stab to the back
She can feel herself slipping into the black
Betrayal of people who aren't meant to hurt
But still treat her like a piece of dirt

She's slowly slipping away
No one wants her to stay
They say go away
Without realising they're not just ruining her day

They're ruining her self-esteem and life
Will they ever put it right?

Lily Sutton (14)
Esher CE High School, Esher

Do Our Best For The Earth

A polar bear is sleeping peacefully at night,
On a tiny surface that you can barely call ice,
Our planet's getting warmer, and we've polluted the air,
To all the animals, is it really that fair?

In a woodland, a hedgehog shuffles by,
Surrounded by tree stumps and grass that is dry,
Animals' homes are being destroyed,
And soon, this will be hard to avoid.

For humans, animals are just there for us to use,
For testing beauty products, and for food,
So, when you see cosmetic products on your phone,
Just remember that animals have lives of their own.

There's still a bit of time, so we can do more,
To save all the animals, and the planet of course,
Let's be more environmentally friendly, and show our worth,
To try our best on behalf of the Earth.

Sophia Hammond-Aziz (12)
Esher CE High School, Esher

Endangered World

The polar bears are dying,
the ice caps are crying.

The rainforest burns,
and the animals are turned,
to sadness and great dismay.

In the future my children will say,
"Mum, what's a great ape?"
and I'll have to say,
"Nothing, they're all gone."

So do all you can,
make a wonderful plan,
even if it's just by turning off your fan,
so now that cray can live to see another day,
hip hip hooray,
now it's your turn to save the day.

Millie Gannon (12)
Esher CE High School, Esher

He's Coming Back - It's Not The End Of The World

He's coming back - it's not the end of the world
The cold of many a winter night
Has found home in both my fingertips and my head;
Chipping away at memories of you - like a chisel to an ice block
There are pieces missing
But with time
And patience
It will form something flawed; yet beautiful-
In its own twisted, raunchy way.
I have found you now; I know where you are
But I shall not give in; I shall not make those steps
However much I may want to.
Your hands are blurry and glitched in my mind
But nonetheless; they are still there
But I refuse to let them
Yank me around
As a puppet on your strings
Anymore.
We were both hurting;
And because of some choices
I still am
But you don't need to know that.
You have ruined me

And I mourn a childhood I never had;
Yet you have also allowed me to flourish.
I changed myself - at first so you wouldn't recognise me
Should I pass you in the street -
But now I do it for myself
I don't want to conform, I want to be me -
Whoever 'me' really is
And
I have met and lost people
But you allowed me to recognise
When to
Just
Stop and think
And you are a part of me, and always will be,
A fact I once resented
But now I have grown because of you,
And once again
I am starting to hate that fact a little less.
The memories are fading,
Our ice sculpture is melting
Yet my feelings towards you are stronger than ever before
And towards myself too
We are one another,
Bound by those puppet strings, though I cut
And cut them
They cannot completely be severed.
And

Once again,
I'm beginning to accept
That if you must be in my life
You don't have to be banished to
The shadow of a burden on my shoulders; weighing me to the floor
Instead;
I can now allow you
To be a part of who I shall become.

Carmen McLellan (17)
Exhall Grange School, Ash Green

Music

Music has this effect on me,
Like magic, something unreal -
It drinks my blood and makes it water,
Takes my breath and makes it breeze,
Embraces my bones and makes them dance
Upon a faraway island in my imagination.
Forever shall I let it possess me
Just one more song, I promise -
And once it's over
I can sing its lyrics
And still feel it deep
Within my bones,
Within my heart.

Juhi Gajjar (16)
Kings Langley School, Kings Langley

World Away...

You lure me up.
Like a sparrow's wings you empower my flight,
Helping me to eclipse safely into the night;
You guide me.

And now when I gaze at you beyond the skyline,
Tracing my mind for some way to convey
Nothing rises.
So instead my fondness disguises,
The yearning desire to cross the border,
And to let the space between us grow smaller.

I'm chasing you.
As you finish blazing through the day;
I'm over the horizon.
Hidden half behind the clouds,
Half wishing to do you proud
Though, you never see me shine.

So I pull the tide,
It's waves in my stride,
Every eve I trace the globe.
But all I hope,
From the top of the highest slope, to the bottom of the sea.
Is that my sun would come down,
And finally notice me...

Those will ponder why the moon still chases the sun.
They forget that love is not attained by everyone.

Lauren Roseberry (15)
Merchant Taylors' Girls' School, Crosby

Pain

Life is pain,
the crime, the fighting, and the corruption,
they decay the Earth every day,
I, too, was in the world of pain.

One day, a light shone on my life,
and had changed my life forever,
slowly, I was turning from bad to good,
every single day.

But, one day, due to the world's decay,
the light was taken, never to be seen,
again.
And I was back to the world of pain.

Abel Sawyerr (12)
Murray Park Community School, Mickleover

Stronger Together

Back in the day years ago, when your grandparents were only kiddos,
Racism wasn't frowned upon; in fact, it was encouraged onwards to the little ones.
The voice of a black person would be muted and prosecuted.
Obama's voice wouldn't have mattered, to be honest he would have been battered.
People would start war over countries, religions and just simply the colour of someone's skin.

Now we're in the 21st century, racism tossed into the bin.
Black people can finally have an opinion and aren't just white people's minions.
Instead of being pushed away, invited to come and stay.
Black people and white people have united together and now we realise we're stronger than ever.

Lily Pinkham (12)
Newquay Tretherras, Newquay

A Call To Arms

We should live in a world of kindness and care,
Instead we live in a world of destruction and neglect.
Hunger, poverty devours humanity,
Diseases spread everywhere
This is the Earth we live on
Because destroy it is what we have done.

All around us nature is disrupted
Glaciers melting
Sea levels rising, towering over us,
Corrupted.
Habitats devastated, don't you find it upsetting?
Yet we stand here, watching our home collapse, but still do nothing
This is the Earth we live on
Is that really what you want?

Look up, the sky cries out concealed by our waste
Oceans are covered in blankets of plastic,
Yet they don't feel comforted by their embrace,
But under threat of being consumed by our 'harmless' antics.

And the car you drive around all day,
Only pollutes our planet's face.
This is the Earth we live on
Small actions cost a lifetime, we still haven't won.

It's a wonderful phenomenon - organisms sprouting into trees
Like we sprout into skilful adults
With every passing moment, these lives are lost
Poor trees scream in pain
No one hears them but the wind, thus we must give them a voice, a chance,
an opportunity to be free.
A change will come with me, you, we.

This is the Earth we live on!
Step outside, explore your surroundings
Take action - to harmful irresponsible deeds stand up, Disallow
Turn off the lights, even the taps
Small steps can lead to new findings
The future is yours, you are the next generation
Do everything you can to help fight this increasing desolation.

Theodora T
North Cestrian School, Altrincham

Empowered

My hood fills with rain,
Your words are down to all this pain,
It feels like my life is swirling down the drain,

The things you do, they hurt me too,
But if I did that to you then you'd feel hurt, wouldn't you,
But when you do it, I use deflection,
And that helps me with my own protection,

But now the tables have turned,
I'm on top of you, I didn't let you win,
This glowing, I feel it in my skin,
It's proudness, happiness, it's empowerment within,
You were the bully but now I'm the king,

Now when I walk home, I don't fall to the floor,
You can't hurt me, not anymore,
Now things have changed, not like before.

Kiera Strathmore (11)
North Cestrian School, Altrincham

I'm Happy To Be Me!

I'm happy to be me,
I love my personality,
That's what describes me.

We may come from a different country,
But we are all free,
The bus boycott in Montgomery,
Shows that we all have responsibility.

Now do you understand,
That I have a demand,
That we can give each other a hand,
And then, we can make this a very fair land.

Angel C (13)
North Cestrian School, Altrincham

My Definition Of Love

What is the definition of love?
Love isn't just a word
It's a feeling of happiness and joy
It comes with so many emotions to express how you feel
But when it comes to my definition of love it's different
It's Her.

Love is as pretty as a flower ready to bloom
Love is a sweet melody ready to be played in the summer
Love swings her hair like a model giving me butterflies and shivers
Love is a foghorn ringing in my ears
Love is a volcano ready to erupt with so many feelings
It's Her.

Taylor (16)
Northview House School, Kilbarchan

The Day That Bravery Came To Visit

Bravery pulled up outside my house in his tank
He rang the bell and knocked heavily
He had special ops armour and a gasmask
He looked dangerous
When I saw him I felt terrified
We had a sleepover and played laser tag
Bravery won
Bravery eats war and drinks fear
Bravery salutes as he flies off in his plane
He reminds me of family.

Zayden Vaughn Sharp (13)
Northview House School, Kilbarchan

The Day Love Came To Visit

Love skipped down the street saying hello to everyone
They knocked lightly
They were dressed in pink with pink sparkly eyes
And handed me a flower
When I saw them I felt overjoyed
We went to a pink party
It was joyful
Love eats a cupcake and drinks sunshine
Love hugs me and blows a kiss goodbye.

Teigan Maria Davidson (13)
Northview House School, Kilbarchan

Little Brothers Are Memorable

He is a small, smiley jack in the box
He is as smart as my Maths teacher
When you look in his blue eyes it's a world of love
And motivation
And a bright future.

Deri-J
Northview House School, Kilbarchan

Hidden

I have hardly been discovered,
I am space
I doubt anyone intends to
Yet every day people learn more
And less becomes a mystery
Each time a new fact is discovered
I am less powerful
I am less hidden
Whatever you discover
Whatever you understand
Whenever you come you leave with another mindset
Whichever planet you leave you return with your mindset on another
The more you know
The less you understand.

Ava Breed (14)
Northwood College For Girls (GDST), Northwood

Love For A Daughter

His face full of sunshine
Each time I come in sight
My cheeky smile and weird laugh
Can bring him such delight
My silly tears can make him smile
But my sad eyes break his heart

The reason for the life he leads
"I play a vital part"
He will slay dragons, swim seas
Or even move mountains for me
No love can be as strong as ours

When I am down he will come around
And fight the blues away
My cheeky giggles are the best sound
But he hates when I go away
He hates to admit it but he loves my company
Oh, and he loves my cuppa tea

His face full of sunshine
Each time I come in sight
My cheeky smile and weird laugh
Can bring him such delight
My silly tears can make him smile
But my sad eyes break his heart

Alexa-Jane Calver (15)
Orchards Academy, Swanley

Butterflies And Moths; Crows And Doves

People have compared us and/or we compare ourselves,
For what? For something society told us was 'the best' or 'the most'
Yes, they may be those things but it doesn't mean you are any less.

We've been told which humans are
'Butterflies'
'Moths'
But in reality,
Both are graceful and beautiful

What did they do to deserve what they are labelled to represent?

One loves flowers
One adores lights
Both are still beautiful
But both can still blind you

And in those species of butterflies and moths, people still look for 'the most' beautiful wings
And in those wings, they look for 'the best' colour and patterns
Broken wings are ignored instead of helped
Others are degraded instead of appreciated

No matter what 'category' you are labelled in
They will keep looking

Ignore them,
Don't listen to their harsh criticisms about you
'You' as a person they don't know or understand about
And they won't bother to
You know yourself better than they do

Those people may see you or won't
But you will be only focusing on yourself and on the ones you care about
Because you found your own happiness
Even if you couldn't find your own happiness
Those judgements won't either
If it beats you down, when you're at your lowest
You will always be there for yourself even if no one else is

Other people hurt you,
Not knowing what you've gone through in life
If they walked in your shoes
They wouldn't be able to survive it like you do
Because despite the pain, don't stop fighting
If you do,
Not only can people get in your defences
But this also allows those awful things control your mind
So start fighting for yourself.

They compared doves with crows
And crows with doves
When they're both birds with different colours
Why is one death and why is one life?
One can see any type of bird
And receive bad luck or good luck
Luck does not rely on what colour birds you see or saw

We are all different and nothing is wrong with that
We can be the same and nothing is wrong with that
People's perspectives and views change
Your perspective can be altered
Opinions can be different
Minds can change

But your life remains your own
Not anyone else's
Keep looking at the bad things
And that's all you see
Start seeing
looking
and finding the good things
And you'll see...

Dana Balao Schoener (16)
Orchards Academy, Swanley

What's The Difference?

Imagine your home being destroyed,
Your family being hunted down,
To know in your dying breath that
Your children are going to be the ones who suffer more.

This is happening to animals everywhere
Their habitat is being destroyed more and more every day
They are being hunted one by one,
Yet you don't seem to care

Humans and animals
What's the difference?
Why do we all carry on,
As if nothing's happening?

Something needs to change,
We all need to change.
We all can better ourselves
To make our world a better place for all

I believe that can happen
If we all make a start
To become more sustainable
We can make the changes Earth deserves.

Chloe Gregory (15)
Orchards Academy, Swanley

I Will Be Like Me, It's My Time

No, they say
No
You will not be like us.

You can't do that.
No one said you could do that.
Stop that.
You can't do that.

Yes, I say
I won't
I
Will be like me.

Oh, but
And I laugh
Oh, but I am doing that!
For it is my time now

I will not look like you
I will not sound like you

For it is my time in the spotlight
You've had yours, move over

I will not pray like you
I will not curse like you

You can't do that
You yell
As you do just that.

I will not love like you
I will not hate like you

Because I
I
Will be like me.

No one said you could do that.
But then again,
No one said you could do that.

Go away!
You scream

Let us live!
I sing

Stop that
Stop what?
Stop that which you do?

I will be proud
I will be disappointed

I will be happy
I will be sad

I will be loud
I will be quiet

I will be free
I will be caged

But I
I
Will be like me.

You can't do that.
You know what?
You can't do that either.

Not anymore

I do not need your approval
I do not need your disdain

For it is my time now

I do not need your love
And I do not need your pain

Because I
I
will be like me.

Regardless of you
I
Will be like me.

For it is my time now
Move over.

Emma-Jane Langley (13)
Orchards Academy, Swanley

Can We Fit Into One Box?

Yes, I know we are not the same.
And even though we have different names, we are alike.
Alike in wisdom which ages beyond our years,
Alike in kindness we share to our peers,
Alike in the tissue absorbing our tears, I tell you we are the same.
We may not have the same colour skin,
We may not all let the lord saviour in,
Nor me or you have the same sized chin, but I tell you we are the same.
All of us can face our fears,
All of us can volunteer, volunteer to be better.
We can all come together as one,
Help each other till our fingers become numb, and make a change.
We can break those lines society has drawn
Help that old man mowing his lawn, and make a change.
Make a change now before it's too late,
Before that homeless man is begging for scraps off your dinner plate, make that change.
We can put those guns down once and for all,
Prevent those horrid 999 calls, calls for help.
Those cowards dressed in designer gear,
The helpless children lying in fear, together we shall change.
Now that change has occurred,
And to some this may all seem absurd, but we have changed.

We have broken the sides in society,
We have helped those kids with anxiety, I tell you we have changed.
No one is outside of my box,
No one has to go without warm socks, my box has expanded.
Expanded to let culture in,
Expanded to acknowledge our sins, a forever change.
A forever change that fits everyone in my box.

Tamzin Doody (16)
Orchards Academy, Swanley

Tables

Tables can be big,
Tables can be small.
Tables can be all shapes and sizes,
Tables can be unique!
So can you.

Tables can be good,
Tables can be bad.
Some tables can be broken,
All tables are grand.
Just like you.

Broken tables can be fixed,
Although some are beyond repair.
The best medicine is laughter,
And friendship a bandage to seal the cut.
Friends are those by your side no matter what happens.

Don't worry about the others,
All tables are unique.
Tables can match,
But it's what's inside is what matters.
And personality counts.

Tables; tables have uses,
Some for art,
Some for smaller kids.

But all tables are useful,
Each with talent.
Like me and you!

Unluckily, tables can turn,
The bumps in the road,
The skin that burns.
Some tables are fake, we don't mind them,
We pick ourselves up and stand tall again!

Annabelle Law (11)
Orchards Academy, Swanley

I Thank You For What You've Done

I thank you for what you have done,
Through all of the tough times you were there,
Always there for me to talk to,
We had our ups and downs but you were always there,
No matter what life threw at us we never gave up
It's all thanks to you,

I thank you for what you have done,
You cared for me and protected me,
I couldn't imagine life without you there,
You helped me through my fears,
Even though some may have brought tears,
You were always there, you never gave up on me,

I thank you for what you have done,
I thank you for the life you provided for me,
How you loved and cared for me,
I thank you for everything...

Ruby May Gomm (12)
Orchards Academy, Swanley

Destined For The Best

Destined for the top
You can make it,
All you must do is strive,
Work until you have reached the top,
There are no checkpoints as we never stop,
Keep working and you can feel free and amazing.
You can make it,
You try and try to get to where you wish,
Never back down, never give up,
The only way to make it is to not stop,
Don't stop believing in your dreams,
It can be what it seems.
Think about the outcome and the future that it may behold.
You can make it,
Become the person you've always wished to be,
Forget the bad times,
And think of what could come up ahead,
You are destined for greatness.

Lewis Walford (12)
Orchards Academy, Swanley

Empowerment

When you scroll on your phone,
On your bed, in your home,
Wishful for their figure,
From just one picture.

Hopes and dreams,
They don't see behind the scenes,
How I wish to look like that,
Rather than feeling ugly or fat.

Insecure, so easy to feel,
They are a rose, I'm an uncared for daffodil.
Horrible thoughts, I hate to think,
Holding back tears, I just have to just blink

You are perfection, you have a beautiful face,
No matter your size, or your style or your race.
It's okay to not be happy all the time,
It's all part of your empowerment climb.

Azaria Peverley (11)
Orchards Academy, Swanley

You

Imagine switching bodies with somebody,
Because you feel like a nobody.

But being a new you,
Doesn't feel like the old you.

People finally starting to know who you are,
The old ones you knew had gone far.

But being a new you,
Doesn't feel like the old you.

You miss the old you,
The person you once knew.

But being a new you,
Doesn't feel like the old you.

Be yourself,
Be you.

Because being you...
Is that the best thing you can do.

Because being a new you,
Couldn't even compare to the old you.

Isabelle Carter (13)
Orchards Academy, Swanley

Empowered

- **E** ncourage your friends to be amazing like you are
- **M** otivate others through your supportive ideas and creativity
- **P** ositive thoughts and feelings help you to succeed
- **O** ptimism will help others to be successful
- **W** isdom will help you make the right decisions in life
- **E** nthusiasm changes the world
- **R** eassure those around you that need it most
- **E** mpower others around you to be the best version of themselves that they can be
- **D** evelop your self-confidence to reach your goals.

Rebecca Jones (12)
Orchards Academy, Swanley

The Truth

You are enough, you are needed, don't ever feel like you're misleading
You're imperfect, that makes you beautiful, you are nothing but useful
You're like a song; you have a meaning, your alluring smile always beaming
Being different isn't bad, in fact, lots of people find it particularly rad
Think of yourself, it doesn't make you selfish, it makes you flourish
You are always relevant and so is everyone else.

Demi Fisher (12)
Orchards Academy, Swanley

Football And 2020

None
Football, we love you,
Gone
Football, we need you.
The world of football came to a pause,
The fans were hoping it would return soon.
They missed the feeling of scoring that goal!
Beating your closest rivals in the biggest match of their lives!
The beautiful game,
We were fighting to kick Covid-19 away.
We wanted to bring football back home.

Ronnie Webb (11)
Orchards Academy, Swanley

Be You

B eing different doesn't make you a bad person
E veryone is different

Y ou should be yourself no matter what
O thers like you for you
U nderstand you're perfect the way you are.

Charlotte Loftus (11)
Orchards Academy, Swanley

Be Yourself

It's important to be yourself
Because if you were like everyone else
Life would be boring and meaningless.
But when you are yourself
You can do a lot of things.

Julia Sibielska (12)
Orchards Academy, Swanley

Wake Up
A haiku

The world is changing,
The alarm is blaring, but
We aren't waking up.

Lucy Coulson (15)
Orchards Academy, Swanley

Flames

The flames dance on the charred wood
lighting up the room crawling up the walls,
the heat filling up the room as the cat sat
on the mat.

The chair rocking back and forth as the widow
wept and the baby slept as the sun goes
to bed.

As the widow wept the man bowed
his head as the news was told,
ending one chapter but creating another.

One silent night became the noisy
night, tears of a widow will be heard
as the fire gets ready to say good night.

The fire flickers giving a warning it's coming
to an end, its light a single candle, light dancing
like a soloist performing.

The man walks out, sorrow hanging on his face,
the weeping widow getting swallowed into
the darkness.

Libby Boobyer
Robert Blake Science College, Bridgwater

Hope

Darkness is in anything
Darkness is always active
Like your beating heart
Just with its bad intentions
It's as sneaky as a snake
Covered in a blanket of hate
This blanket tries to choke you
Like it's squeezing out all good
But through the darkness
The moon is bright
Yes, through the darkness
Shines a bright light
See through the darkness
Out burns hope.

Violet Gainsford
Robert Blake Science College, Bridgwater

Change Will Appear

You may be ignoring or joking,
But this is not a laughing matter.
Our world is vigorously changing,
And it is not for the better.

Twists and turns in our weather system,
As gas emissions submerge our globe.
We are the thieves of our ecosystem,
And the consequences are escaping the wardrobe.

The outcome of greenhouse gases:
Severe storms, increased drought and not enough food.
Water levels are above their masses,
And the loss of species is far from good.

The repercussions are on a treadmill,
Going faster and faster every day.
We must climb to the solutions, just over the hill,
They are not a needle in the hay.

We can help, please listen well,
Take a leap and consider your waste.
Use your voice, ring the bell,
You must act now, ambition based.

We can walk, cycle or scoot to minimise the fumes,
Reduce, reuse, recycle and repair.

Don't forget to turn lights off in rooms,
Have your wits about and be aware.

Are my solutions loud and clear?
If we shout loud enough, change will appear.

Orla Fullerton (13)
Sacred Heart Grammar School, Newry

My Bodhrán Drum

My Bodhrán drum so sound and sweet.
Listen to every meaningful beat.
The taught and tuneful kangaroo skin,
Crafted and fastened to the olivewood rim.

Playing in groups, duos and solo.
Keeping the beat with the fiddler's elbow.
Learning, performing, practising with friends,
And the Bodhrán stick clicking at the very end.

Confidence, happiness and pride,
All the while playing a 6/8 slide.
So many rhythms: polkas, hornpipes, reels and jigs,
All of us playing one big gig.

The music travels through your blood,
While your foot taps along with a thud.
Your adrenaline pumping throughout the tune,
It's like flying to the moon!

Whenever I play, no matter the place,
I play high notes as well as some base.
A triplet here and a rimshot there,
I'm never afraid to add a little flare.

My Bodhrán drum makes me feel empowered,
Like a blossom that has just flowered.

Amy Fitzpatrick (13)
Sacred Heart Grammar School, Newry

The Power Of Nature

What inspires me? I wonder,
More than riches or gold
It's the beauty and awe of nature
As the mystery of creation unfolds

The rainbow after the rainfall
The sunrise and sunset each day
The wind lifting leaves in a slow dance
Or the colours of Spring-time displayed

It lifts up my heart and my spirit
To see nature doing its thing
Whether that be the tide ebb and flowing
Or at dawn hearing birds tweet and sing

A climb to the top of a mountain
With a view of the ocean below
I feel like I could do anything
With this body that nature bestowed

It reminds me of what I am able
The nature that lives within me
With gratitude for all that surrounds us
The best things in life do come free.

Aebha Phillips (12)
Sacred Heart Grammar School, Newry

Animal Extinction

Our animals are dying,
Extinct they will be.
It's our problem that we are denying,
Why can't everyone see?

They're losing their habitats,
They're being hunted down,
There is no time for chit-chats,
The jungle has been stripped of its crown.

Climate change is occurring,
Nitrogen pollution is in action,
It all needs a good solving,
We could make it our avocation.

Prevent soil erosion,
Dispose of your waste properly,
Support a helping organisation,
Think your actions through carefully.

Together we can make a change,
In keeping our animals alive.
Even if our lives have to rearrange,
They deserve to survive.

Amy Fullerton (13)
Sacred Heart Grammar School, Newry

Our Tomorrow

I am melting away, drowning myself
I am being held captive, struggling to breathe
I am kneeling down, minute after minute
But no one seems to notice what is wrong with me
I am changing day after day
I am mostly water and land
I am getting closer and closer to my extinction
All I ask of you is for a helping hand
I am inching and inching towards the end
I am irrelevant, at least that is what many people seem to think
I am important and needed in this life
But once I'm gone, you will realise that I am unique
You and I are very alike
There is one of you and one of me
I am your home
Your only chance at life
I am the Earth
Can't you see?

Kate Boyd (13)
Sacred Heart Grammar School, Newry

Memories

Relaxing on a sofa,
With all my friends too,
All having a laugh,
I cannot feel blue.

In an old kitchen,
With nice people around me,
Delicious food everywhere,
Romanian style... yummy!

In a painted church so cosy,
Singing our hearts out,
With smiles on our faces,
Our friendships sprout.

Even somewhere faraway I can call Dublin home,
The place where love taught me I can never be alone.

One day I will leave that beautiful place,
And there will be tears streaming down my face,
But then I'll remember the wonderful memories,
Which are my most treasured accessories.

Iulia Zanfir (13)
Sacred Heart Grammar School, Newry

Who Is Equal?

I grew up believing we stood as one in harmony
But the self-segregation and little education
Has caused conflict in society

It doesn't matter if you are black, white or brown
Just know to hold up your crown
If we stand hand-in-hand
We will soon understand
How important we are all around

No matter your background or race
We are all in the same place
So pick up your mic
Tell Malala she was right
"Even one voice is powerful!"
So stand up and be cheerful
Everyone is equal.

Cara McCusker (12)
Sacred Heart Grammar School, Newry

My Cat, My Pearl

Tiptoe, tiptoe in the snow
as gentle as a butterfly
She is a stealthy, slinky silhouette
in the silent light of the moon

Eyes sparkle and twinkle
like diamonds in the dark
She is my cat, my Pearl
and she is special in my heart

The wind blew fast and wild
whooshing like a swirling hurricane
She is a shooting star in the night
in the roaring storm she shelters

Eyes sparkle and twinkle
like diamonds in the dark
She is my cat, my pearl
and she is special in my heart.

Kate Orr (13)
Sacred Heart Grammar School, Newry

It Will Get Better

It will get better.
My ideas have been shot down before,
Not been given a chance,
The constant sting of rejection,
Denied the opportunity to advance.
It keeps me up at night,
The reoccurring rebuff,
It plagues my mind,
Am I just not good enough?
I wouldn't wish this on anyone,
This burning frustration,
Never know if you'll succeed,
Reaching new levels of exasperation.
I can't wait for this to be over,
To finally be accepted,
These feelings will leave me,
I know it'll get better,
The pressure will ease,
But until then I'll work hard,
And do my best to appease.

Morgan Bonnage (13)
Sir Frederick Gibberd College, Harlow

Being United

Being united is stronger than being divided
Through race, age, culture, gender, or ethnicity
United is a word that brings us to be one
If we are divided there will be no brightness

The light is the key to the doorway of success
The darkness is the key to determination
Success is the way
Success is our gain

The spirits of our ancestors
Were never divided
And always united
By race, age, gender, culture, and ethnicity

Bring the world together
As one not millions!

Caitlin (14)
Sir Frederick Gibberd College, Harlow

Empty

I drop my flowers at the grave,
I can see his face with his clean shave,
As tears roll down my cheek,
I remember how it felt when he would brush them away,
And that's when I know I won't love another day.
I was left in darkness,
As you were not there to light the way,
I made some choices I regret,
I wish I wouldn't live another day.
My home doesn't feel the same,
So, I sold it,
And I know I am to blame,
But I had to get rid of the memories,
That caused me such pain.
I am on the streets in a pit of despair,
I am shivering as my back is bare,
Tears roll down my cheeks,
I feel trapped,
I have been here for many weeks,
I am devastated,
I am homeless.
Food wrappers litter the floor,
And I wish I wasn't too poor,
As it feels so close and yet so far,
I wish that everything would be destroyed just where we are,

All the lights and music fading away,
All turning to rubble around me today.
Looks of disgust etched on their faces,
As they stare me down, I imagine the places,
That I could be in this devastating life,
Yet instead, their stares pierce me like a knife,
I wish that he was still alive to help me through my struggles,
My dear husband would give me power through his cuddles,
But I am alone in this horrible world,
Where children look down at me,
And an old, hungry woman is all they see.
Why is this still here?
It has been hundreds of years,
I have lost all I hold dear,
And yet homelessness still runs rampage,
I feel trapped as if I am locked in a cage,
I need help.
We *must* stop homelessness!

Niamh Magee & Claudia Tombaccini-Maestro
St George Catholic College, Swaythling

A Recipe For A Better World

Ingredients:
Kindness
Integrity
Love
Respect

Method:
1. Add two large cups of kindness,
As this will remind us,
That on a bad day, we will be okay,
And in the darkness, it will find us.

2. Then, sprinkle in some integrity,
Who cares about popularity? What we need is solidarity,
And morals to help us act disciplinarily.

3. Next, a few heaped tablespoons of love,
Which should be added with a good mix,
For a hug or a kiss, definitely outstrips,
The nasty comments in all these conflicts.

4. And finally, a pinch of respect,
Accept and protect everyone's individuality,
Let's interconnect to make this planet perfect.

Rosie-Anna Prior (13)
St James' CE High School, Farnworth

Unstoppable

Women hidden by men,
defined within walls that never fall.
Freedom far, far from reach,
but yet those who are in power could push down.

Flowers bloom inside,
trying to escape,
but yet still hidden with thorns
scraping till the final scrape.

Each vein carrying hope,
that leaves as the branches
of our happiness snap.

All women begin to lose,
not only their hope but colour,
as the sun, the clouds and sky fade.

We wake up, we fight!
We work, we fight!
Yet the sexism, the comments still carry on.

There is no limit to what we as women
can accomplish.
We overcome the winds
that makes us unstoppable.

This makes us unstoppable,
unstoppable today, tomorrow, next week,
forever.

Melissa Bailey (13)
St James' CE High School, Farnworth

Take The Plunge

No peace lives in my mind,
No thoughts ever surrender
And in that way I am forever defined.
Myself, my biggest offender.

I preach of peace and stopping war
But I often find myself on the other side of the shore,
A hypocritical man who wants so much more,
Left stranded by everyone to be done for.

I wonder. Looking at my thoughts as they crash against each other like a strong, thrashing ocean
Forever surrendered to one long-lasting motion.
Swaying into the shoreline, flooding it with emotion.
Will it ever stay still if I have enough devotion?

The thought of it finally stilling is brought on by a thrill.
A thrill brought on by you waving at me
Upon your boat floating with self-will.

I stand upon my ocean's shore looking out yonder,
Wondering how you're not scared to drown in my own ponder,
As I know I am and that's why I never wander,
But for you I'd drown a thousand times just to see you look at me with any remnant of honour.

My icy blue eyes finally melt as it meets your warm brown
My face that is usually carved melancholy with a frown
Is suddenly undone and is turned upside down
And even the war surging on around us begins to come around.

You begin to draw closer, a wave of hope swelling in my chest,
It hits and hides the rough dark rocks of my life's unrest.

You're getting even closer, our souls practically touching,
Mine reserved only for you and your cherished retouchings,
I feel myself become selfish, my hand now out reaching
Out for you, your hair, your eyes and your smile which are quickly approaching
But as you do I feel myself diminishing and my waves begin ambushing.

I'm not the peacemaker you so dream of
I'm an ongoing hypocritical war,
That you somehow still manage to love,
Though I don't know what for.

Your boat begins to crash against my own violent waves,
But you continue somehow, never wavering from brave
How could you love an ongoing fight and how can you wish to save,
A man whose only power is to be imprisoned and enslave.
It's all I can think about as my body starts to cave.

For if I am the sea, you are the moon,
A bright shining light contrasting to my dark lagoon,
The only hope in my life,
That I soak up all too soon.

I finally raise my head up from the coast,
Desperately trying to shout for the host of your boat,
But my vocals are trapped by the mauling of the sob stuck within my throat.

Were my waves finally too much for you,
Just as the sun was when Icarus flew?
Too dangerous and destroying for anyone, no matter their power to get through.
So destroying even the man who meant to control them got overthrew.
I'll never know now, as you've disappeared into the drowning blue.

Quiet droppings of sea salt fall from the sky,
Though as they wander down my face I know they come from the corners of my eyes.
The cause for them either your demise or my down despise,
But something cuts them off and takes me by surprise,
It's you, swimming and thrashing deep within my ocean's battle cry.

I won't let myself swallow you up,
I know the danger of myself as I live in its constant disrupt
The way I get up is quick and scarily abrupt

Though I don't worry about that as I meet the edge of my overflowing corrupt,
I look at it for one last moment before my feelings finally overtake and erupt,
Too long trapped and scared to shout and interrupt.

I plunge into the thrashing of my thoughts,
No longer frightened as I'm overtaken by my feeling of immense distraught.

I no longer care about the sea around me,
As I swim and swim for you, reaching and grasping your hand, desperate to be set free,
My mind disagrees with my sudden emotion-filled spree,
As it can finally touch and see,
But my heart beats with glee,
The image that is you
My beautiful, beautiful Makkari.

Niamh McCann
St John The Baptist's College, Portadown

Something Important To Me...

Something important to me...
How do I find out what something means to me?
How do I decipher my loves, my losses,
My emotions?
No.
When everyone surrounds,
Screaming, scolding,
Why do adults think this is the way?
No.
I know what I want,
What I like, what I love.
I know what I want!
What I dislike, detest,
Reading my thoughts,
Projecting them onto the world;
The world of wonder,
Wonderful hope.
Can you hear me now, world?
You won't tell me what it's like to be me;
This is me.

Holly Preshur
St John The Baptist's College, Portadown

Ask For A Smile

A mask,
it restrains us to a pair of eyes
we can see others
but can they see us?
We can feel and look one way
but how are we really?
The blue abyss that is now half of us
but at least there is no lockdown though?
Wrong!
You can not see a smile
you can not see a glare
behind all of this, we are alive.
Ask,
you will receive
are you okay?
That day, you might shed a tear
you might feel rage,
but the question is are you okay?
Some say have a bath in sage!
That will help relieve the stress.
Just ask,
that's all we need to cause a smile,
doesn't cost a penny,
only a word from the heart

Ask for a smile,
that will make my day.

Olivia Groark (13)
St Robert Of Newminster, Fatfield

Empty Shell

It all starts with a snigger.
Then you know.
Initiate shut down.
Block out the world.
The waves rise.
Tie down the mast.
Hatches secure.
Ocean swells.
Takes control.
Turn.
Walk.
Splinters cascade.
Ship still intact.
Don't watch.
Don't turn.
Don't talk.
Make an empty shell.

Mathilda Warren-O'Neill
Stockport School, Stockport

Why?

Why?
Why should I not go outside in the dark?
Why?
Why should I be scared to walk on my own?
Why?
Why should I keep away from other people?

Everybody should be able to speak to whoever
they would like.
Everybody should be able to go outside whenever
they would like.
Everybody should be able to walk with whoever
they would like.

When will we get equal opportunities?
When will we get equal pay?
When will we get equal lives?
When will we get equal rights?

Just because the government said so,
doesn't mean everybody does.
Just because the rules say so,
doesn't mean everybody does.
Just because people think so,
doesn't mean everybody does.

I want to go outside in the dark
I want to walk on my own
I want to talk to other people
I want
to be equal.

Erin-Lily Taylor (13)
Stockport School, Stockport

Dear Future Self

Dear future self,
Do you walk the way you used to before?
Remember when we were a kid and we ran barefoot on the open shore,
Do you now run in shoes afraid you would step on stones
Silently hoping that the now sharp rocks would leave you alone?

Dear future self,
I feel fear and power portray your eyes.
A mix of emotions in your hidden disguise,
Hope is evident and shown in different ways,
Hope is in your eyes and I feel time flies once again.

Dear future self,
Do you have the same angry power?
If someone hit you would you hit back harder?
I required that empty questions would mean nothing without an answer,
If you were Santa's reindeer would you still be Dancer?

Dear past self,
Oh how naive I was,
Do you this and do you that, you will never know when to stop asking that,
Yes, I run in shoes and I'm still described as lame,

I love Dancer but Dancer is acting up recently what a shame,
Doesn't dance like they used to.
That's what they claimed
But would we still look back on our memories and think the same?
Oh how naive you are,
Let's hope and hope till we can't get enough,
Laugh and laugh until our belly hurts.
You never know when the next time will come,
That next chance you'll get might fade and become numb,
Depending on your action so choose wisely.
For now, let's run freely

So let's laugh and laugh
You act so daft
You're are stuck in the ol' good times,
Oh past self,
What are these lies?

Let's just enjoy ourselves
We only have one life,
Make the most of it!
This is real life.

Storm Rogers (14)
Stopsley High School, Luton

Fasting, Fasting

Full moon rises till then I start,
Full moon sets till then I fast,
Days last so long,
Yet nights so short,
But in the name of God, I keep fasting, fasting,
Some try and some finished,
Some try but are forgiven,
I try and try whilst seeing people eat,
As I am constantly starving to my feet,
Coming close to the food, knowing I can eat when I break soon.
I try and try, since there is no lie, no lie.

Full moon rises till then I start,
Full moon sets till than I fast,
For 30 days or maybe less,
For these days you are blessed,
When the moon is thin but still,
Till then he and she will,
When I watch people eat it is hard,
But still I try my best, knowing this makes me,
Even though eating seems so far,
In the name of God, I keep fasting, fasting

Here is one of the five pillars,
Now here comes Eid,
So here is to the ones who know.

Eid Mubarak from Eid al Fitr to Eid ul Adha, so here's to all who love the Islamic religion.
But when the full moon rises till then I start,
Full moon sets till than I fast,
In the name of God, I keep fasting, fasting.

Ali Kayani (14)
Stopsley High School, Luton

In Our Own Way

Learning to love who you are can be difficult
You might look in the mirror and say
"Why don't I look like them?"
But you have to realise that
Every curve, spot, freckle and dimple,
Makes you, you.

You open up social media and see
Skinny, 'flawless' models living life freely
They exercise and eat kale willingly
You may think their lives are perfect,
But you have to realise that
They cover up a lot of things
They don't want you to see.

Now more than ever we talk about our mental state
Social pressures and norms dictate
How everyone should look
Like we should follow an example from a book
They preach perfection
But you have to realise that
It would be a shame,
If everyone was the same.

You might struggle to love who you are right now
But give yourself a chance,
To discover your worth

You have to realise that
Nobody is perfect,
We are all different,
We are all special
In our own way.

Milly Hawkins (14)
Stopsley High School, Luton

My Fate Isn't Told

Everybody syas I'm weak
and need to perfect my fatigue
they say it entwined fate
and that's something you can't change.

But in reality
I don't believe in fate
only I carve my path
and don't believe in wrath.

No one is right
no one is wrong
who knows what this world holds
and so my fate isn't told.

People can push me down
and tell me I'm wrong
and judge me wrongly
as they compare
but I don't know or so much care
because not everyone's judgement is fair.

Only I hold the power to my fate
no one else
people are judged
and often thought of as wrong
but I don't

I'm strong in body
and most importantly
strong in heart.

Safiyyah Jarral (12)
Stopsley High School, Luton

Maybe

Maybe it's because they're jealous
Maybe it's because they're rebellious
Maybe they will be the one that saves you
Maybe they might think you aren't the one for them
Maybe you're their Wonderwall
Maybe they want you to play ball
Whatever they want it needs to stop
Maybe they wanna be yours
Maybe they want you to watch Star Wars
Maybe they love you
Maybe you're their best friend
Maybe this needs to end
Maybe they need to skip a page
Maybe they have the urge to lock you in a cage
Maybe they need a hug
Maybe they need to be loved
Maybe they need a kiss
Maybe just maybe they need a friend.

Mia Stratton (12)
Stopsley High School, Luton

What If?

We all stand in a line
Different shapes and sizes
But that won't matter in the end
As we will still get judged for shape and size.
"You eat too much," he says
"You don't eat enough," she says.
But what if I just didn't care what others think?
What if I only cared what I thought?

We're told you have to do this to be perfect
We're told to wear that to be perfect
We're told to eat this to be perfect

But what if I stopped caring about what people think?
What if I only cared about what I thought?
What if I was more like Jo March
Living my life the way I want?
What if I was more like these women I read about?

Iris Bartlett (13)
Stopsley High School, Luton

You Can Do Anything

You can do anything,
You can be anything,
You can see anything,
You can dream about anything,

If you can think it,
You can do it,
No matter who you are,
Where you are,
Or what's happening around you,
If you can dream it,
You can do it,

No matter how big,
Or how small,
As long as you have the will,
The drive,
The determination,
The right mindset,

You can go above and beyond,
Prove the impossible possible,
Rise above the rest,
And be the very best,

Whatever happens,
We can all do amazing things,
You can do anything.

Aryan Uddin (13)
Stopsley High School, Luton

Find Yourself

Soul desires, eyes dither
Who are you eager for?
Waiting with bated breath.

If nobody responds, you move forward
Alone...
If no one heeds your call, then
Walk alone...

If the whole world turns its back on you,
You turn your back onto the world
And speak out your mind, as loud as you can!
You bare your soul and find your freedom.

With all severe pain, purify your soul
Following the accompanying clouds,
That float towards the far horizon.

You shall silently reside, and
Take a look inside your heart;
Surely you will perceive your soul.

Tahsiath Tanmi
Stopsley High School, Luton

N'Golo Kanté

From worst to the best,
It's all about strength.
Black is power, black is history, black is everything
Back in the past, black didn't mean anything,
From New Guinea
And everyone in-between,
N'Golo Kanté, from rags to riches,
Always worked hard, cleaning streets and then on football pitches
It's how you pick yourself up,
Not how you let it affect you
Bin man to world-class baller,
A perfect example to making yourself better,
You should always respect one another no matter what race,
Even if the challenges are the worst you have faced
Kanté, Chelsea CDM, French World Cup winner,
And a beloved human being.

Luke McCulloch (12)
Stopsley High School, Luton

Answer Me

What is the distinction between you and I?
Your life and mine?
Reality and lies?

You are delusional,
You can not see.
You're behind my bars.
Only I set you free.

Do you see those pixels?
That is your life.
You are my fair maiden.
You are my wife.

It better not be,
My trust that you lack.
I will smile at your face,
But put my cig out on your back.

I built your land.
I receive many likes.
Your eyes are blurred.
Unlike mine.

Do you understand me?
Yes, you do.
You want me, you crave me.
I'm what you'll always choose.

When will come the day,
That you finally realise,
I have you, I own you.
No reality, just lies.

Anushka Patel (14)
Stopsley High School, Luton

Feminist

Confidence,
Be your own person,
Don't change yourself for anyone,
If you think you're beautiful,
You're not the only one.

Feminism,
We should all be treated the same,
Judge me as a person,
Just because I am a girl,
It shouldn't become a game.

Love,
Don't settle for the minimum,
Be treated as the queen you are,
Wait for the right person,
Raise a high bar.

Happiness,
It's something we all need,
Let yourself have fun,
Let yourself lead.

Sophie Croft (14)
Stopsley High School, Luton

My Religion, Islam

Islam is my religion and it inspires me to wear the hijab.
Every day I wake up to pray five times a day.
Maybe sometimes I'm a let down, but I know I'll get back up again.

Islam is my religion and it inspires me to fast,
Ramadan is what you do till your religion day (Eid).
The day you can eat is after thirty days.
This year Eid will be the 2nd of May.

I now know what to do or not,
My religion has inspired me to do a lot.
It's hard to believe that all of this is just from my religion.

Aliyah Hoque (11)
Stopsley High School, Luton

Friends

From a young age
You will always have someone
You trust them
You play with them

Over the years
You'll lose some
Make new ones
You care for them

You gradually become an adult
You have that same someone
Through thick or thin
To become the best person ever

You're at old age
You've grown old with them
They pass away
People there to comfort you

People think they know loads about them
You're in their will
You became their family over the years
That one person has changed your life forever

That one person
Is your friend forever.

Lexie Dawson-Mannion (14)
Stopsley High School, Luton

Dear Future Me

Dear future me,
Hopefully you have done well in your GCSEs,
Always work hard and try your best,
But also make sure to take a rest.

Dear future me,
Spend time with your family,
Because they come first,
Your family will always be there for you,
But make sure to play a joke on them and go, "Boo!"

Dear future me,
If things are hard right now,
Don't blame anyone else and get into a row,
Always think of the good things,
Like when the lunch bell rings.

Ava Mensah-Mahmud (12)
Stopsley High School, Luton

The World

The world would be a nice and happy place to be if everyone listened.
It would be nice
If everyone listened the world would not suffer.

If everyone listened the future generations wouldn't suffer.
If everyone listened the young people wouldn't fight for their lives!
If everyone listened I wouldn't have to write this.
If everyone listened I'd ask them to be environmentally friendly.
Help us, recycle,
Be friendly to the place you live in.
Don't destroy it! Save it!

Tahsin Sayed (12)
Stopsley High School, Luton

Education

School tries to make me happy,
But at the minute,
It's making me the person I don't want to be.

School was something I looked forward to,
But now it's,
Something I hate to think about.

My friends,
The smiles,
The memories we have had,
Makes me never want to lose these people,
Because of the laughter we have had.

The homework every week,
Piles up,
All the teachers care about
Is the money and how to 'succeed'.

Aimee Thrussell (12)
Stopsley High School, Luton

Moving On

Moving on,
Leaving this life behind me,
I'm achieving my dreams by,
Leaving this life behind me.
My hopes, my dreams,
I'm following them by,
Leaving this life behind me.
I'm taking control of my new life,
I'm leading my new life by,
Leaving this life behind me.
You inspired me,
You encouraged me to go,
So I'm leaving this life behind me,
I'm moving on,
I'm moving on by,
Leaving... this... life... behind... me.

Evie Keeling (14)
Stopsley High School, Luton

My Culture, I Think

My culture's my background
My eyes
And my hair
My culture's my why
And my when
And my where
In places
And faces
And skies up above
My outside, my inside
What I'm thinking of
The country of my fathers
Where born was I and raised
Of the nations I move to
And spend most of my days
The village
The city
The food and the drink
What makes me special?
My culture, I think.

Pawel Doruch (13)
Stopsley High School, Luton

Thank You

I come to you when I'm sad
I come to you when I'm seeking motivation
I come to you when I'm being doubted
And that person is Conor McGregor.

You prove people wrong
You overcome adversity
You love to prove people wrong
And your name is Conor McGregor.

You showed me the law of attraction
You showed me to believe in myself
You showed me to not follow others
And you are Conor McGregor.

You are my hero
You are my idol
You are Conor McGregor.

Kam Reid (13)
Stopsley High School, Luton

Class Of 2022 Graduation Speech

To the class of 2022...
Good luck with the hard future you will have.
You might start a business that will open shops across the world,
Become a famous YouTuber that will make a lot of money every day,
Become a teacher of Stopsley High School,
Become the prime minister of the United Kingdom,
And you might become a professional footballer that is known across the world.
Good luck in your future.

Ibrahim Hossain (12)
Stopsley High School, Luton

Empowered

- **E** mpowering others
- **M** akes me happy
- **P** eople inspired and feeling overpowered
- **O** thers feel invincible like me
- **W** hat makes you feel better about yourself?
- **E** veryone can be inspired, just wait and see
- **R** eally, inside they can be hurt
- **E** ven you, at times, could be
- **D** oing our best to overcome the bullies is the best thing for me.

Mahad Haider Afsheen (11)
Stopsley High School, Luton

Ants

Pittering, pattering
Staggering, navigating
Down the path
Between leaves and trees
Down the hole
Into their humble abode

Carrying grains
From higher plains
Carrying leaves
Filled with an abundance of food
Carrying corpses of foes
Lingering with woes

Down the hole
Into their homes
Off they go
Filling their treasure trove.

Eshan Hussain (12)
Stopsley High School, Luton

It's Okay

Hoping you're doing well
Just like to say it's okay to be scared, it's okay
Look back at the mistake you made
It's okay to be you
People say it's bad
Some say you don't fit in with the crowd
Well let me tell you something
Those people are scared or ashamed
So don't worry what people say
Because at the end of the day you're happy.

Alonso Mangwende
Stopsley High School, Luton

Powerless

Dear world,
I don't know what to say.
If only I could change you,
But here I lay,
Feeling as powerless as ever.

Dear people,
I'm sorry I let you down,
But I tried my best,
Still here I lie powerless.

Dear animals,
How do I save you?
I think to myself,
What did they do to you?
And I am still here living powerless.

Alecsandra Ciolan (11)
Stopsley High School, Luton

A Teacher For A Week

Waking to school, a very nice stroll.
Nothing to make me panic until the children roll.
Walk through those gates, I am not ready.
For the children will come, I will not be steady.
English, first lesson, here I am.
Maths, next lesson, last time I ran.
The children come rushing in, ready to say, "Here, sir."
And I will teach them, because I am a teacher.

Alex Chapman (14)
Stopsley High School, Luton

Dreams

You are going to have and probably had a dream,
Maybe you wanted to be an astronaut or prime minister,
Well you can do anything!
You may tell people your dreams and they laugh,
Well don't give up!
You are special,
You are unique,
You are strong,
All you need to do is believe!
I hope that you look back and see,
Your dream became a reality.

Olatomiwa Osobu (12)
Stopsley High School, Luton

My Sister

Every day I'm with you.
I see you every morning till night,
Even though we fight you still mean a lot.
You help me when I'm sad,
You help me when I need it.
What would I do if you left?
You've helped with homework,
You helped me to get where I am.
We listen to each other's day,
Now it's my time to work hard like you!

Iqra Islam (12)
Stopsley High School, Luton

About Myself

Roses are red
Violets are blue
I know about myself
What about you?
If you don't know me
I will tell you
I am kind
I am caring
When someone's sad
I make them happy
I can cook
I am funny
I am gonna tell you
What I love
I love art
I love horses
I love my family
And that is all
About me.

Katie Davis (11)
Stopsley High School, Luton

My Best Friend Diana

Day after day you inspire me,
You make me happy and have a big smile on my face
Making me laugh,
Comforting me when I am sad.

Day after day you inspire me,
Whenever you play football
I want to become as good as you,
Even if it takes an eternity.

Day after day you inspire me,
I appreciate you and what you do for me,
I hope we are still friends,
I will never forget you.

Nikola Dadia (13)
Stopsley High School, Luton

Colours

Thank you,
You've shown me red,
You get in my head,
And show me how to dream.

Thank you,
When I'm feeling blue,
You wait for me when I tie my shoe.

Thank you,
You're my white,
Like a light,
You're my angel.

Thank you,
You're my brown,
You never let me down.

Maja Laclak
Stopsley High School, Luton

Trust Yourself

My favourite thing about myself is my skin and life.
In every person's journey, they have all been through strife.
Times may be hard and a bit negative at parts which hurts us in tears.
But the way you are is the way you appear.
Love yourself and don't change anything about you.
Trust yourself, this is true.

Kiyana Henry (12)
Stopsley High School, Luton

Good Morning, Everyone

Good morning, everyone
Come and get ready
Good morning, everyone
Come and get steady
Good morning, everyone
Get your equipment out
Good morning, everyone
Get your books out
Good morning, everyone
Come and sit down
Goodbye, everyone
See you around.

Freddie Theron (13)
Stopsley High School, Luton

Mushroom Souls

You helped me bloom,
Just like a mushroom,

You helped me grow,
And so I shall glow,

You helped me be myself,
My true true self...

You make me laugh,
You make me smile,
You make me happy,
Every day,
Every day.

Mia Larsen (11)
Stopsley High School, Luton

Sky

I'm the light after night
I am Sky when I cry
I bright light in the world
That's why I am called Sky
When I die, when I die
Then there is no sky
That can cry
I die every night
I rise every day this way
I am Sky, Sky, Sky.

Hasnain Qaisar (12)
Stopsley High School, Luton

Dear Future Me

Dear future me,
Did I make it?
Dear future me,
Am I still fit?

Dear future me,
I can't wait for summer.
Dear future me,
Did it thunder?

Dear future me,
Did I speak?
Dear future me,
Was I too weak?

Emily Booth (12)
Stopsley High School, Luton

Meows

Whose cat is that? I think I know
Its owner is quite happy though
Full of happiness like a beautiful rainbow
I watch him laugh, I cry no more

He gives his cat a shake
And laughs until his belly aches
The only sounds that break,
Of distance meows and birds awake.

Ehsan Hanif (14)
Stopsley High School, Luton

What Is School?

I ask myself this question more times than I should.
It's a question not many people can answer.
Most people say something along the lines of:
"It's a place to learn skills to help you in life,"
but I don't understand what skills I can make use of.

What about maths? Taking x and y
and "use the quadratic equation to find them."
Or finding a missing angle in a triangle,
when given all the others.
Or figuring out the vector by which a shape has travelled.
Maybe "find the coordinate where the graph starts to level."
"What transformation maps B onto A?"
What does this teach me?
"It teaches you to solve problems on your own,
something that'll be very useful later on."
Oh, okay. If that's what you say.

What about English? Analysing extracts from novels,
and writing four-page essays on
"How is this character portrayed in this chapter?"
But having to come up with our own ideas to get more checks
on the mark scheme list.
Because thoughtfulness is key.
Taking apart a quotation and looking at each word's hidden meaning.

Like how 'The door was red' clearly symbolises the pain and suffering
felt by the protagonist.
What does this teach me?
"It teaches you to come up with creative ideas and how to think outside the box."
Oh, okay. If that's what you say.

Six hours of work is enough.
But then we have to do another two at home.
And teachers wonder why
none of us get a good amount of sleep.
It's because we stay up late on our phones
because we couldn't after school,
or we stay up late doing homework or revising
because we just have too much.
And we can't always follow this rule.
"Homework is a very useful tool,
it'll help you further understand the complicated things."
Oh, okay. If that's what you say.

We get detentions for forgetting homework or being late
just because we were in a rush, or we slept in, or the bus was late.
What happened to second chances?
What happened to extensions?
Why do you skip straight to detentions
if we have never put even a toe out of line before?

Why punish us for mistakes we make once in a blue moon?
We are all human at the end of the day.
"It's about discipline and time management."
Oh, okay. If that's what you say.

Truth is, some skills learnt will be useful down the road.
Like finding discounts off of clothes
or interest in my bank account.
And knowing the difference between antiviral and antiseptic
will help me when I'm sick.
But the majority is just to be memorised and spat out onto tests.
And then have us guessing at the percentage amount.

These tests will decide our future college,
where we learn things that will actually help us.
But it seems unfair for our futures to depend
on a number on a piece of paper.
What if people aren't good at memorising things?
What if they can't "figure how much he will have to spend"?
What if they can't "make X the subject of an equation"?
Too bad. Try again later.

Hannah Jones
Stretford Grammar School, Manchester

In The Void

A child so sweet - maybe 13 or younger,
Left to rot away from the cold and from hunger.
Many people decide to pass them by,
Leaving without giving, and only a repulsed look in their eye.
This child is so weak, bones cracking and frail,
No shelter is given to them, for sleet and for hail.
Charity is not enough to save them from their demise
For there are thousands of children like this, waiting for their prize.
Our little wealth alone will not help them become healthy,
The people in white houses are already plenty wealthy:
They have lots to give, and yet do not share,
Narcissistic men and women spending gold just for their own flair.
Prioritising their life and petty 'needs' before others,
Oblivious to struggling families, fathers and mothers.
They feel no remorse when they tread on poorly people's feet
And gorge on costly wine and exorbitant meat.
If there is enough to overfeed the pampered and the spoiled,
Why isn't there enough for those who are living in a void?

Emmy Smith (12)
Stretford Grammar School, Manchester

Change

Growing up we are taught to live in perfection,
Everyone must be greatly similar, no change of direction.
We are praised for our unique achievements, that is if we match a certain description,
That we are the 'right' size, the 'right' race, that we share the 'right' reflection.

But tell me why we are taught that it is wrong to be different,
If our qualities aren't the 'usual', we are seen as a predicament.
But if we are seen to be the 'correct' way,
Our change of the system is praised, is that really all that sane?

We must believe certain beliefs,
We must see eye to eye, we must make ends meet,
No! What we really must do is change this hierarchy,
Not the one we can earn our place, but the one where our rights aren't taken away
Because of our race.
And that we see an end to our remarks being self-obsessed and snarky.

So, we must change what we preach,
Our younger generation can't be forced to believe

To believe that our looks, our background, our religious views,
Are a sight to be laughed at, to be wrecked and abused.

We must stop this now, now while we can,
Before too many other lives are sacrificed because of those who can't understand.
We must stop this now, no time to hesitate,
We must stop this now before it's too late.

Sophie Allen
Stretford Grammar School, Manchester

It Is...

It's easy to feel powerless
when we have no say in the elections,
when a corrupt government
forces a rule onto us and yet
breaks it when they think we aren't looking
"one rule for you, another rule for us"
but it won't stay like this forever

It's easy to feel powerless
when hundreds upon thousands of companies
dump plastic in its millions of tons in the sea
destroying ecosystems
endangering animals
and their punishment is nothing at all
but it won't stay like this forever

It's easy to feel powerless
when millions of people in 'developed countries'
still go without meals,
without a home,
and those with the power to change it
are completely content with it
but it won't stay like this forever

It's easy to feel powerless
when those older than us
are so quick to put us down

"You're all just kids!" they say
"Your minds haven't developed!"
as they do nothing about a crisis already upon us
but it won't stay like this forever

And even if nothing changes
even if we make no difference
at least we actually tried
at least we weren't blinded by our egos
at least we recognised there were injustices in the world
while you lot sat there and did nothing at all.

Ben Carroll (15)
Stretford Grammar School, Manchester

The Legacy Of Your Name

You always did walk the halls with your head held high
under the gaze of unwavering eyes
misery held beneath artificial smiles
yet your facade never did break,
not a single crack.

For the image they had created
emitted light expelling the black,
loneliness filled your aching heart.
I never did understand.

How you continued,
knowing you were doomed from the very start,
you knew. That was the price you had to pay:
coerced 'I'm fine's, programmed 'okay's,
manipulation was practically their middle name,
innocent sailors lured into their unruly game
in which they demanded a siren.
You had seemed the perfect candidate,
many falling under your spell.
Alas, your mind became theirs,
foreseeing the devil's bidding until the very end.

Until.
You shut their eyes,
they were blinded.

You covered their ears,
they were deafened.
You, ever-so-perfectly flawed.
Your to be, ever-so-perfectly planned.
You knew. Your mind was never theirs.
Drizzles of manipulation never did settle,
for you cannot beat the devil at her very own game.
Their fruitless torments, you overcame.
How I wish to follow, the legacy of your name.

Aya Yousif
Stretford Grammar School, Manchester

Them

The street lamps were fuzzy halos,
Brightening the path up ahead,
The path of success they called it,
Struggling along the road, the made me walk upon,
I fell into an abyss of darkness,
I tried to reason, but
It was my fault - so they said.

They make me go to school every day,
It's meant to be good for me.
The path of success they called it.
Trying to remember equations, formulas; why John Snow was so significant and keeping my mental health in line too.
I fell into a mental abyss of darkness
I tried to reason, but
It was my fault - so they said

They said I need to be like them to fit in
Look a certain way, act a certain way, lock myself away.
The path of success they called it,
Trying to be accepted by society, fit into their moulds and be myself at the same time,
I lost myself in an abyss of darkness
I tried to reason, but
It was my fault - so they said.

Living in their world, living by their rules, I lost myself on the path to success.
I fell into an abyss of darkness
Which I never woke up from.
I didn't try to reason, but
It was still my fault - so they said.
Leaving the fuzzy halos to be consumed by darkness.

Bisma Rizwan
Stretford Grammar School, Manchester

Curiosity Never Stops

You may say I don't know
But I have a long way to go
In school, I will thrive
And at home I will surprise
My parents with my knowledge
As I'm eating my morning porridge
Over time, there will be many paths that I choose
But I have nothing to lose
And all to gain
But some of my attempts might be vain
Not to gain money
As that will only increase my greed
But to gain opportunities to do a good deed
I always try to succeed
But it isn't guaranteed
To learn is my goal
And my goal is to learn
Ever since my life started
Until the day I will have departed
From this world
Into the unknown
Which I always want to know
But remember, this hasn't happened yet
And don't forget
I still have a long way to go

So don't say that I don't know
Because you don't know that either
And I will become an achiever
You might think I'm not smart
But I still have belief
And I will work hard to become the golden leaf
Meanwhile, you stand there in disbelief
I have said this many times and I will say it yet again
So please refrain from saying I don't know
Because I have belief and a long way to go.

Daniel Ghebreyesus (12)
Stretford Grammar School, Manchester

A World With Solutions

Shuffling along through every street,
Rivers of smoke amongst frigid sleet,
We cough, splutter,
They cry and weep,
This is a world with no solutions.

We could hear the cries,
We could help,
We could aid the sky,
We could clean its tears,
We could eradicate the smoke creeping near
We could, we could, we could.

Some are forced to learn to shrink, to hide,
Some can break the mould, and challenge the thoughts inside,
We walk amongst graves touching endless cold,
We can't live without fear, but we can be bold,
Every day is about surviving,
And to continue thriving.

We can hear the cries and help,
We choose not to aid the sky,
We can eradicate the smoke,
We choose not to spread our wings and fly,
We can, we can, we just have to make that choice.

Minds and voices free, birds swirl and fly,
Every breath pure,
Happiness fills the sky,
The sky weeps in happiness,
For the ground beneath is whole

This is a world with solutions
This a world for the next generation,
This is a world worth those choices,
It is possible, plausible, potential,
We have to open our eyes and see.

Minahil Hussain (13)
Stretford Grammar School, Manchester

For You, My Dear

Bring your winds to wave me goodbye,
for I don't know if I will return, let the winds carry my regards,
let me take you with me, to feel your presence when I'm lonely.
When I fear the unfamiliarity of the passing breeze - to purloin you away
for my heart and my soul will stay here with you, as my home is with you.
Once I settle in the boat, promise to remember me -
even if I sink,
even when we plummet,
even if we drown,
as you are all that's left behind.
I am sorry I ought to leave, it's hard to disagree with destiny.
The colours of your smiles seem so vivid in my mind,
now they rage in the fires and darken in the rubble,
your music once filled the streets that now roam bare and cold.
You are still there but no longer remember me for you have forgotten yourself.
You let go of peace,
let go of pride.
Patriotism,
a concept you've forgotten.

A kiss of salt on the corner of my lips
and it takes me back to the day you let me go.

Jouna Albaid (17)
Stretford Grammar School, Manchester

Empowerment, What Even Is It?

Empowerment, what even is it?
Authority and power given to someone to do what they please.

Quite often placed wrongly in the corrupt hands
of the megalomaniac global elite.

But, oppositely, placed in the hands of rebels
who believe their views are correct,
or given to regular people like you.

Reader, the power will corrupt their tiny brains,
but me, I'm different,
I am a billionaire nomad.

Empowerment in my hands would allow the fit to flourish
and the lazy destitute to die,
those who are addicts to banned substances,
will perish and those with nothing,
through no fault of their own, will live.

The homeless, the hungry and the thirsty,
will be blessed, for they shall inherit my fortune,
but the criminals of our Earth,
the murderers and petty thieves

who are locked away and forgotten about
will be dealt with once and for all.

I am an idealist,
not unlike Cassius and the Caesars of the top
1% will meet the same fate as him.

William Murphy (15)
Stretford Grammar School, Manchester

Lingering

Lingering in every corner,
Lurking in every street,
A lethal foreigner,
Silent and discreet,
Poaching our dear family,
Like a hunter out for blood,
We must quench this agony,
Bring fury like a flood,
They call themselves our government,
Yet all we've accomplished is nada,
They call themselves our government,
Yet even the prime minister had a
Party whilst his people were condemned to
Self-imprisonment in each of their houses,
So disgusting how they have no clue,
That people are dying in the thousands,
Now back to the reason for the poem,
Those fools in power must be eradicated,
So by next year we will throw 'em
Out of power, our resolve radiated,
I will need your aid to fulfil this fearsome feat,
Those senseless dictators must fall this age,
And now to make our hearts complete,
We must escape this bloody cage.

Divine Chijindu Udensi (15)
Stretford Grammar School, Manchester

Six Letters

A word with six letters, it's something you can't buy
There's not enough money in this world, you'll appreciate it till you die
A word with six letters, it'll make you feel empowered
It'll help you when you're devastated, it'll make you feel appreciated
A word with six letters, whatever could it be?
It makes you feel on top of the hierarchy
The word with six letters? The word is friend
Friends help you when you're down, friends are there 'till the end
You make memories and you make bonds
Together you're as strong as diamonds
Sometimes you don't see them anymore
Sometimes they'll move across shore
Nevertheless, the bond will not be broke
Because we'll be friends until we croak.

Fezaan Ali Hussain (14)
Stretford Grammar School, Manchester

Global Warming

Global warming,
The weather is storming,
I'd say it was a good morning,
But the rain won't stop pouring.

Look about,
The endless drought,
You hear the shout,
They can't get out.

Elsewhere, there's floods,
Overflowing swamps of mud,
Nothing but a destroyed neighbourhood,
Tell me, how is this good?

While temperatures are searing,
The ice caps are disappearing,
People are fearing,
This is the direction we are steering.

The sea levels rise,
Now, it's no surprise,
You hear the cries,
How the time flies.

The damage we are causing,
It's so appalling,

Humanity is falling,
But together, we can stop global warming.

We need to make change,
Our habits rearranged,
Stand up, be brave,
I'm begging you!
Our world, our Earth, needs to be saved.

Mariya Alam (14)
Stretford Grammar School, Manchester

How Can We Believe It?

"Nobody's perfect," it's what they all say,
but how could we believe it, when the world is this way?

Everyone has bad days,
and that is a fact.
But when nobody presents that,
how does the fact stay intact?

Daily, we see,
people's wonderful days
and you think, *how do they*
have it their own ways?
When it seems like your world
is a total nightmare
but your friends have fun,
like they don't care.

How can you keep,
the attitude you're taught
when people party in lockdown
and don't get caught?
Their lives must be a dream,
this is what you believe.
But how can they blame you?
That's what they want you to see.

"Nobody's perfect," it's what they all say,
but how could we believe it, when the world is this way?

Eva Carpenter (14)
Stretford Grammar School, Manchester

To The Future Me Who I Will Always Love

Dear future me,
Though times may be tough,
Hold on to what is steadfast,
And remind yourself that you're enough.

Dear future me,
When horrors get to you,
Just remember that someone will always care,
And will be there to carry you through.

Dear future me,
Though life might be pain,
Remember to smile
And think of what you will gain.

Dear future me,
Never lose hope,
When times get tough,
Just remember to cope.

Dear future me
To one I'll always love,
Follow your dreams,
And fly high like a dove.

Dear future me,
Dark times will end soon,
So continue on,
To the moon.

Dear future me,
Just remember,
That I'm with you always,
And leave you I will never.

Dear future me,
Always remember,
I'll love you always,
Unto forever.

Favour Osuagwu
Stretford Grammar School, Manchester

Education Evolving Your Future

Something new is given to mind every day
A new treat to tease the tastebuds and create curiosity
Learning keeps us awake for this day
And excited for that day

School keeps us occupied for the week
Makes sure our mind isn't weak
And is thinking at its peak
For we never know when our life may become bleak
So we need the brain to keep those words from our lessons
In the purest detail

Something new springs into our thoughts
Every hour of those six hours
Every word from our teacher may spark new ideas
They teach us to respect our peers
And keep thinking clear

Education lays the stepping stones to our future lives
The question is
Are you ready to take that path
And live the life you always desired?

Education empowers endlessly.

William Boast Kemp (13)
Stretford Grammar School, Manchester

Colourful People

We are people made of bright, bright colours,
Our skin, our soul, our mind.
We are all full of bright, bright colours,
So let's leave our inequalities behind.

We are people made of bright, bright colours,
We come from wide and far.
This doesn't make us strange or different,
It just makes us who we are.

We are people made of bright, bright colours,
We all express ourselves
Every day, in every way,
From first hellos to last farewells.

We are people made of bright, bright colours,
We have limitless imaginations.
Never will we cease to continue,
Filling life with glorious creations.

We are people made of bright, bright colours,
We each love who we love.
And we are who we are, whoever that is,
Nobody, no one, can stop us.

Lola Heys
Stretford Grammar School, Manchester

Don't Give Up, It'll Be Alright

Don't give up, it'll be alright,
Everything will fall in place, it's worth the fight,
Primary school may have seemed tough,
Though high school, it is a little rough.
It's just how it goes, it always gets harder,
But through the struggle, your spirit grows larger.

Many friends wait here, experiences and all,
Life is only more fun when you're on the ball,
Always join in, enjoy your time,
I'd crawl over rocks, scale mountains, climb
To savour that sense of carelessness.

Primary school might be easier, more fun
High school's also filled with laughs, it's not a pointing gun,
Don't look down, hold your head with great height!
Everything in your life, it's looking bright.

Yazan Naser Eddin (13)
Stretford Grammar School, Manchester

A Message To The Girls

To the girls who keep every sentimental gift,
To the girls who walk home with keys gripped between their fists,
To the girls who smile at strangers in the street,
To the girls who can't help but watch what they eat,
To the girls who love to read books in the park,
To the girls who fear for their life in the dark,
To the girls who love with all their hearts,
To the girls who wish they were known for something other than their body parts.
I hope you know that you are loved by so many in the world,
I hope you never, not even for a second, question your worth.
You're beautiful,
You're strong
And you're empowering
And you make everybody's life that little more exciting.

Sofia Ahmed (16)
Stretford Grammar School, Manchester

She Can

She can stand up for herself
She doesn't listen to "she can't" or "she won't"
She can do whatever she wants
She doesn't listen to "you stop" or "just don't"
She can be as strong as she wants
Without being bossy, cruel or vain
She can feel however she wants
Pleasure, anger, sadness or pain.

She can learn anything that she wants
In any way that she needs
She can look however she wants
And she doesn't have to please
She can live however she wants
And she can choose her own path
She can think for herself
She can fight. She can cry. She can laugh.
She can care.
She can dare.
She can be.
She is me.

Olive Broom (12)
Stretford Grammar School, Manchester

Thank You

Someone who takes the time to think of other people's needs,
and warms our hearts with their thoughtful deeds.

Someone who volunteers to chase depression away,
and add a ray of sunshine into every day.

Someone who - to the best of their might - tries,
to understand, support and sympathise.

Someone who's always eager to share,
and to help and give and smile and care.

It's never dull to have someone beside you with a beam,
they always sees a silver lining and makes life seem like a dream.

I think this is a fantastic chance to tell you too,
that the world would be a much better place if more people were like you.

So thank you.

Shaker Darwazeh (14)
Stretford Grammar School, Manchester

The Power Of Women

Remember you are stronger than you think you are.
You have the power to bloom open your blue colours.
Forget the suffering that scars.
Have the courage to let kindness in this world of decolour.
Let peace heal the wounds that the heart conceals and don't
look back at those memories that cut through
like shards of glass.
You need to realise that you are free
to dress up for work or carve out a life for yourself.
There are no restrictions to how you choose to live your life.
You are not alone.
You are confident and an
inspiration that deserves to be recognised.
Nothing is possible in your absence!

Kainaat Wahid (18)
Stretford Grammar School, Manchester

My Best Friend

He was a boy
Who would try to talk to me
Who brought out my joy
And made sure I stayed happy

He became a friend
Someone to lean on
Who'd tell jokes on end
To ensure my negativity gone

He would be there by my side
Cherishing my company
Someone who'd be there when I cried
To always comfort me

Now he's my best friend
Turning ultramarine blues into radiant yellow
Who's there for a benevolent hand to lend
Being the sweet centre of a marshmallow

He's like the stars in the night sky
The umbrella in a storm
I thank him for making the days fly by
And for being my supportive platform.

Syed Ibrahim Ali (13)
Stretford Grammar School, Manchester

Future

The future is bright
Let's hope I'm right
I'm in the past
So don't think too fast

Think of me well
But try not to be too swell
You should have tried hard
And been dealt the better card

Think about what you've done
And always make life fun
Keep busy with hobbies in your life
As it will keep you out of strife

Always love your family and pets
And try your hardest not to rack up any debts
Get on with people in a group
And keep up with the loop

The future is in your hands
So take opportunities to visit many lands
If you want to be smart
Now is a good time to make a start.

James Swales (14)
Stretford Grammar School, Manchester

To My Future Self

To my future self,
I know I haven't met you yet,
I imagine you as strong and powerful,
A kind person who helps those who are upset.

To my future self,
Though we are years apart,
Never to cross paths,
I wish you all the best at your new start.

To my future self,
I hope you remember those who have helped you,
I hope you recognise their faces in the dusty picture books,
And don't forget them to make room for those who are new.

To my future self,
Although you may face trouble,
And long, hard times,
Remember the times that were fun as the present, past and future is invaluable.

Scarlett Moss
Stretford Grammar School, Manchester

Twilight

Silver birch shadows, drooping yet tall,
Fades the brightness of their line.
The mountain, small, lean and stronger,
Grasping onto the earth below.

And the clouds creeping westward;
Fleeting as nature descends
Upon valleys, deep in purple sleep.
All the sky is crimson wine.

Broods a mist of amethyst
Individually each sunbeam gracefully falls
Now the silhouette of hills;
On the sky's forgotten glow.

Bringing glamour to this evening
With the stars and crescent-shaped moon.
Among many of the creatures drifting to sleep
Daylight finally rests, as twilight effortlessly depletes.

Dhillan Nagra (14)
Stretford Grammar School, Manchester

Hope For Our Countries

Countries falling tomorrow, today,
There's just a few things I'd like to say,
The days of war are miserable and long
However, as one we'll stand up strong,
Try your best to share your love,
There's no need to fight, push or shove,
Listen to the rules, do what's right,
Love all countries,
It will pay off, trust me,
Help those who are needy and poor,
Your help will open many doors,
We should love our families with all our heart,
We should all do our part,
Afghanistan, Iraq, Somalia, Syria, all need help,
Their people are in need, we need to help.
We need to help.

Subhanullah Naseri (13)
Stretford Grammar School, Manchester

Loving You

I never thought we'd go
But I guess that's how every story flows
You were a princess in a tower
I was an ogre every hour
I rescued you with my armour and sword
But I was no good-looking lord
I know you could have chosen any destiny
But you don't know how thankful I am
That you saw the best in me
And I know these people could give you diamond rings
But I'll give up anything
And I'll still never know what to do
'Cause all I know is
I was made for loving you.

Rory Kielty (15)
Stretford Grammar School, Manchester

World

What is going on in the world?
Tension arises,
As the smoke swirls.
To us, the world despises?

In the world, what good is there?
Friendship, happiness, love and comfort.
The world can be fair,
If we put in our effort.

The world can make you happy or sad.
It can put a smile on your face,
Or make you mad.
Our job is to embrace the world.

To me, the world is a gift,
Which we can't open until the end.
So we should have fun until we drift away.

So what I'm trying to say,
Is that for me, the world is great.
Getting better day by day.

Saahil Malik
Stretford Grammar School, Manchester

The Deep Abyss Of Space

Into the deep abyss of space,
We discover the unseen.
Finding remarkable beginnings
Of our planets with sheen.

Into the deep abyss of space,
We oppose the limits.
Launching spacecraft towards orbit
In just a few minutes.

Into the deep abyss of space,
We develop new plans.
Habitating astronauts
In space cavity cans.

Into the deep abyss of space
We study every star.
Using high tech telescopes
To see galaxies from afar.

But despite the many years of effort,
With scientists so ace
We still know so little about
The deep abyss of space.

Ivan Flitcroft (17)
Stretford Grammar School, Manchester

Poem To The Person Who Inspires Me

Of the past few months, Covid has come in and out of me
I am now writing a poem to the person who inspires me

To Micheal Jordan
Have you ever met Gordon?
You were a famous ball player
Got a doc on iPlayer

Made your own shoes
They were all on the news
I got a pair myself
They are on my shoe shelf

You were number 23
Landed on your knees
After a goal in the net
And you always won the bet

You're the chairman of the Charlotte Hornets
A business that went enormous
You're worth 1.6 billion
That's more than a multi-million.

Esa Mohammed (12)
Stretford Grammar School, Manchester

To My Future Self

To my future self, have I achieved medals, badges, goals and trophies?
And could you tell me if I have passed my GCSEs and how big are TVs?
Have any of those aliens yet invaded the planet?
And have companies finally invented graphene jackets?
Do I own multi-billion pound companies?
Or am I on the streets begging for freebies?
Or am I the most famous person ever?
And can I actually control the weather?
Hopefully, you can answer these questions without a doubt and one last question,
How much money do I own in my bank account?

Ryan Buckley (12)
Stretford Grammar School, Manchester

23rd

Perched upon a stone wall
Gazing at me with your green eyes
Behind which that I will never know is disguised

You recognise me; I do too
The day I was walking through the avenue
The scent of morning dew in the air
The hairs still stick to my coat
And of your presence they denote

Seems that from my life you withdrew
Nowhere to be seen in your small recluse
Two months and you're not there
I walk past that avenue and my heart despairs
My feline friend for whom I pine
I long for the day your eyes meet mine.

Nadia Basir (16)
Stretford Grammar School, Manchester

To This Generation, Please

To this generation, please
Stop cutting down the trees
You're hurting wildlife, even the bees

To this generation, please
Our Earth is full of pollution
Let's all work together and find a solution

To this generation, please
As humans we should all unite
We should be kind and finish these fights

To this generation, please
We should protect our Earth
As it is a land that's worth

To this generation, please
We should do our bit and don't leave on rest
And our end result will be the best.

Muhammad Tahoor Ali
Stretford Grammar School, Manchester

Stretford Grammar

You were always there for me,
We assisted each other,
We adored what we had,
We appreciate what there was to appreciate.

You were always there for me,
You would brighten up the room,
You would light up my heart,
You were the special one to me.

You were always there for me,
You would influence me,
You would understand how I thought,
You were my saviour.

The light that never stopped shining,
The glue that never stopped sticking,
You were never stopping,
This is why I acknowledge you.

Luca Cardilli-Ferry (13)
Stretford Grammar School, Manchester

Equality

How would it feel?
Feeling scared on the streets?
Worried for your life?
Having the feeling that repeats?

How would it feel?
Earning less than others?
That this injustice still remains?
An injustice here since the time of your grandmothers?

How would it feel?
Being told what to do?
Have to look after a family?
That being the only acceptable way to be viewed?

Why after all this time,
Aren't there complete equal rights?
Why should women have to hide,
And feel they cannot fight?

Daisy Wheadon
Stretford Grammar School, Manchester

Wires

Inside me are wires,
that my job requires,
to connect the components within me.

But the way I am wired,
often makes me more tired,
than the other machines.

The other machines are loud;
whirring away like a restless crowd,
while I am almost always quiet.

The other machines are quick;
getting their jobs done as fast as a click,
while I have a slow connection.

The other machines think I'm broken;
something sleeping that cannot be woken,
but I am just differently wired.

Kira Lee (13)
Stretford Grammar School, Manchester

Books!

When I go to bed I think to myself,
which book shall I read from my bookshelf?
I love all genres from comedy to thriller,
I also love mysteries and finding out the killer.
Inside of a book I always find,
places and people of every kind.
Whenever I read I learn something new:
a new word, new figure, or someone's point of view.
The more I read, the more I know
because books help me to grow.
Instead, tonight when I go to bed,
I'll read something I haven't read.

Hanifah Aslam (11)
Stretford Grammar School, Manchester

With No Home To Go

With no home to go
Walk past me, make me beg
Thinking of this hurts my head

With no home to go
Worn down by life
Knowing that my situation is rife
Weary eyes, tired feet
I feel like I'm in defeat

With no home to go
The night is cold and bitter
Making my whole body chitter
The concrete steps hurt my back
Making all my bones crack

With no home to go
Help me, please
Just give me some house keys
Feed me, give me shelter
That's all I need
Just one good deed.

Jack Styczen-O'Keefe (13)
Stretford Grammar School, Manchester

Educate

When I walk past men
I prefer to be ignored
Than to be smiled at

'Cause sometimes a smile
May not always be friendly
All of us know that

Hold our keys tightly
Never walk alone at night
Never show your skin

But remember girls,
Even though it's *all* of us,
"It is not all men"

"Protect your daughters"
Why can't everyone say,
"Educate your sons"

You can not forget
You guys would not be alive
If not for your mum.

Sofia Whitehouse (16)
Stretford Grammar School, Manchester

A Good Day

A big bowl of breakfast in the morning,
A whole load of chores to do,
A smile from someone you've never met before,
A big hug from someone you have,
A book you just can't put down,
A look at a brilliant view,
A carefully prepared lunch,
A cookie with the perfect crunch,
A talk with an old friend,
A walk with a new one,
A song that you can't help but dance to,
A throng of people to dance with you,
A movie that you love,
A late-night snack,
A good day.

Freya Scott (11)
Stretford Grammar School, Manchester

Beauty Of Nature

In the bushes, in the trees, in the ground
This is where the beauty of nature can be found
From ponds to rivers to lakes to stream
The beauty of nature only one can dream

The birds in the trees, the frogs in the pond
Of which this kind of nature I am fond
Clouds in the sky the sun's warm glows
I even like it when nature snows

I can see the beauty of nature wherever I go
No matter the weather
No matter the place
I will always see the beauty in nature.

Evan Lewis (13)
Stretford Grammar School, Manchester

Memories

My friends were far
But yet so near
Being alone was my greatest fear

I cling onto the remnants of what was once whole
To keep the memories
Our tales of old

Our memories were old
Our memories were young
Abundant in joy and love
But sadness and anger also

Our emotions ranged
From high to low
Where the winds will take us
We will never know

My friends are near
But yet so distant
My fear was gone
And the memories with it.

Reuben Quansah
Stretford Grammar School, Manchester

Educate Your Sons

"Don't walk home through the park," they say;
Educate your sons.
"Don't walk home in the dark," they say;
Educate your sons.
"Wear a longer skirt," they say;
Educate your sons.
"Don't forget your alarm," they say;
Educate your sons.
"Text me when you're home," they say;
Educate your sons.
"Boys will be boys," they say;
Educate your sons!

Erin Mann (14)
Stretford Grammar School, Manchester

Graduation Speech

To the class of 2022,
You have nothing to lose.
These past few years,
Have been something quite new.

To the class of 2022,
The time has come,
For us to go separate ways,
And to fulfil our destinies.

To the class of 2022,
This isn't the end,
It is just the beginning.
Where to go is up to you.

To the class of 2022,
I wish you good luck,
As you have a life ahead,
And I know you'll do your best.

Hibah Khan (11)
Stretford Grammar School, Manchester

To Future Me

To future me,
I know things can be tough.
Through Covid we have persevered,
Through unprecedented stuff.

To future me,
We can make a difference.
Even if it doesn't go our way,
We can turn this into a preference.

To future me,
There are many possibilities,
Many new chances,
New availabilities.

To future me,
We have come this far already,
Let's carry on in life,
Show it that we are ready.

Jack Chell
Stretford Grammar School, Manchester

School

I wake up with a smile
But it'll soon fade
I have to go to school
It's so boring and makes me drool

Now you'll know the pain
School is so damn lame
Ohhh the pain
(Wwwhy?)

Let's face it, school's as boring as gruel
But I know I'll have to go
Otherwise, I'll never learn and grow

And even if I didn't go
I'd have to find another way
To learn and grow.

James Osuh (12)
Stretford Grammar School, Manchester

If I Could Live

If I could live forever
I would take my time
I would do everything over
Until I got it right

There would be no urge
No rush nor care
Everything by please
No risk or dare

I would have no stress
Because everyone would soon be gone
And I'd be a lonely mess
With forever to waste

There would be no cause
No reason to try
So would forever be history
Or just forever misery.

Harrison Ritchie (15)
Stretford Grammar School, Manchester

Holiday

Hold on, hold on
Chairs on just one leg
Hold on, hold on
We are all on edge

Hold on, hold on
Sun blaring through the glass
Hold on, hold on,
Time is so slow to pass

Hold on, hold on
Bored faces all around
Hold on, hold on
The teacher's voice is the only sound

So close, so close
All we want to do is play
3... 2... 1...
Finally, it's the summer holiday!

Laura Goodyer (12)
Stretford Grammar School, Manchester

Build

Lego, what to expect,
imagination is free.

An endless pool,
millions upon millions.

Dive right in,
build, just build.

Build what you want to be.

Possibilities infinite,
bricks upon bricks

Build, just build,
build what you want to be.

Lego Ninjago, Lego City,
Lego Star Wars, Lego TNT.

It is what you want.
Build, just build.

Build what you want to be.

Benjamin Hosford (12)
Stretford Grammar School, Manchester

Climate Change

The smoky skies, the horrible air
The people on the planet don't seem to care
Clear skies and beautiful days are never seen
The world nowadays is never clean
Inspect what's happening in the world
The cars, fires and pollution
Hopefully, we can find a solution
We need to raise awareness about this situation
Because this can ruin our land and nation.

Sihaam Omar (13)
Stretford Grammar School, Manchester

Plastic Pollution

The nightmare of nightmares,
Its footprint scours the ocean,
Leaving a deadly mark for the nature that is to come.

Birds, sharks, turtles, and more,
Washed up on the beach,
Dying, more and more.

However there is a solution,
To remove this terrible pollution,
Once and for all,

All I can say
Is one simple word,
And that word is,

Teamseas.org.

Syed Younus Hussain (12)
Stretford Grammar School, Manchester

Your Skin

Sometimes you feel
Like life is hard
Uncomfortable in your own skin
Your heart you guard

You may want to conceal
Keep quiet
Hide how you truly feel
But soon you'll learn

Soon, times will change,
You can smile more,
Love to see your face
And once your heart's in the right place -

You can finally be comfortable
In your own skin.

Oluchi Ezekiel (13)
Stretford Grammar School, Manchester

My Idol - LH44

He is brave
He is bold
He didn't listen to the scolds
He is talented
He is unique
He is part of the British fleet
He is a Knight
He shows no fright
He is just like me
Black and beautiful
He showed me who I can be

Sir Lewis Hamilton
Thank you for teaching me
That no matter who I am,
I can ignite the world.

Ronique Walker (11)
Stretford Grammar School, Manchester

To Future Me

Me of the future
Don't feel down
A negative day
Can be turned around

Me of the future
Look forward to your future
Stay outside
Get off the computer

Me of the future
Have no worries
Do some cooking
Make some curries

Me of the future
Look back to the past
Old experiences can help you
To not come last.

Kaj Middleton (13)
Stretford Grammar School, Manchester

Green

As green as the grass,
Green like the trees,
That sway in the breeze.

Green is the colour of new life.
Green is the colour of spring.

However if we go on,
The green will fade,
Lost forever and we can't get it back,
The cost of our concrete jungles.

Let's save what we have left.

Oliver Hitchen (13)
Stretford Grammar School, Manchester

Rain

It races down the glass windows,
plunging into puddles below.
It swiftly slides off the slanted rooftops
flooding the silent streets and rundown shops.

Grey smokey clouds gathered in a cluster
trapping the sunlight like a prisoner.
It creates a melody,
I wonder what it could be...

Zoha Munir (15)
Stretford Grammar School, Manchester

Melt The World

In a world of destruction,
Forests burn,
Ice caps melt
And ecosystems are disrupted.

From the polar bears in the Arctic,
To the tigers in the jungles,
This world is melting.

But we can stop this havoc
Stop plastic use,
Stop food waste,
Solve the puzzle of climate change.

Ben Parsons (11)
Stretford Grammar School, Manchester

What?

What do you want?
What do you do?
What do you read?
What are you doing?
What is what?
What is what?
What is existence?
What is purpose?
What are purposes?
What does what?
What is what?
What is what?
What is what?
What is what?
What is what used for?
What is what?

Muhammad Abdulwahab (11)
Stretford Grammar School, Manchester

Climate Change

The biggest problem we have faced
It only takes a second
To look at which bin you throw your waste in
Instead of travelling by car
Go take a walk or cycle with your friends
If everyone does their little bit
The world would be a much better place.

Cohen Jackson (12)
Stretford Grammar School, Manchester

Dear Future Me

Dear future me,
Don't ever get into
A situation
That
You can't decide
What is truly correct.

Dear future me,
Don't ever forget
What is your own opinion?

Dear future me,
Don't ever believe
That
Others will do your job.

Shaowen Xu (12)
Stretford Grammar School, Manchester

Give Us A Smile

Walking along the road
Minding my own business
He slowed
"Give us a smile, darlin'," he said.

I didn't want to smile
Not for you anyway, stranger.

Georgia Smith (16)
Stretford Grammar School, Manchester

Something

Something to do
Something to think
What shall I do?
What shall I think?
Something might happen
Something might occur
What shall happen?
What shall occur?

Ozzy Thorp (11)
Stretford Grammar School, Manchester

Wandering Souls

The moon split in half
And the stars crumbled,
Falling like fireworks
Into the sea.
I watched my world
Fall apart the day
My hope left me.

Ali Sharfeden (17)
Stretford Grammar School, Manchester

The Journey
A haiku

The path, long, obscure
steps closer with each lone breath
till I fade away.

Ahmed Soomro (16)
Stretford Grammar School, Manchester

YoungWriters
Est. 1991

YOUNG WRITERS INFORMATION

We hope you have enjoyed reading this book – and that you will continue to in the coming years.

If you're the parent or family member of an enthusiastic poet or story writer, do visit our website www.youngwriters.co.uk/subscribe and sign up to receive news, competitions, writing challenges and tips, activities and much, much more! There's lots to keep budding writers motivated!

If you would like to order further copies of this book, or any of our other titles, then please give us a call or order via your online account.

Young Writers
Remus House
Coltsfoot Drive
Peterborough
PE2 9BF
(01733) 890066
info@youngwriters.co.uk

Join in the conversation!
Tips, news, giveaways and much more!

YoungWritersUK   YoungWritersCW   youngwriterscw